# A Winning Team

## The Story of
## Everett, Elmer & Lloyd Nordstrom

## By Elmer J. Nordstrom

# A Winning Team

The Story of
Everett, Elmer & Lloyd Nordstrom

*Cover photo—Everett, Lloyd and Elmer Nordstrom as boys.*

*Elmer Nordstrom*

# Introduction

THIS book is about three brothers, the sons of a Swedish immigrant who started a small shoe store in Seattle. It's about how that store grew to become the largest shoe store in America, and eventually, the country's largest specialty store chain.

It's about the people who helped us along the way, through the lean years of the Depression when we almost lost everything, the troubled war years and post-war growth. Finally, it's about our wives and families who stood beside us, and who have heard more shoe stories than they care to remember.

Writing this book was not my idea. However, occasionally I am asked to speak to our new personnel, to tell them about the old days and the things we did that worked well for us. Many people have suggested that I collect these remembrances and record them as a continuaton of my father's book, "The Immigrant in 1887."

For the most part they are simple things, but it's good to hear about them now and then, so that they're not forgotten. Unfortunately, my brothers aren't here today, so it is up to me to write this book.

I would like to dedicate it to their memory. Here then, is our story.

# Growing up in Seattle

*E*VERETT was born in 1903. I showed up the next year. Lloyd took his time and didn't make an appearance until 1910.

We lived in Rainier Valley which was out in the country in those days. We didn't have electricity, but we did have a cow, some chickens, a couple of turkeys and a horse. The horse pulled a sedan for all of us, or a roadster that looked like a "surrey with the fringe on top." After father bought a car he sold the horse, but we kept the cow. Father milked it before work and mother milked it in the evening.

Father built our house in 1904 when his business was three years old. It sat up on a knoll overlooking ten acres that he owned at Juneau Street and Empire Way. We had four

7

bedrooms, but the whole family slept out on a big sleeping porch, which was rather common at the time. It must have been a well-built house, because it's still there today.

From our windows you could look down on a bunch of smaller houses in the valley. All of them had little houses out in back, since indoor plumbing in the country was pretty rare. One morning I remember waking up and glancing out the window, and there were all the outhouses, resting on their sides. It was the morning after Halloween.

On Christmas Eve, usually around 8:00, my father would tell us he was going to check on the animals. A few minutes after he left, why, in would come Santa Claus. My sister could play the piano so we would all sing carols for quite some time until Santa gave us our presents. Then he would leave until next year. Immediately afterwards my father would come in and we would all say, "You just missed Santa Claus!" This went on for a few years until one day we found a Santa Claus suit up in the attic, and that took care of that.

When I was young, I took some abuse because of the name Elmer. But Lloyd, who was given the middle name of Nels, got most of the kidding. We called him "Nelsie." One night when I was studying at the dining room table, Lloyd came up to me and said that he wished he could change his name. No one else was home, and I asked him what name he would rather have. "Walter," he said. I suggested we change it and he asked how. So I took him over to the kitchen sink, drew a glass of water and told him to place his head over the basin. Then I poured the water over him and christened him "Lloyd Walter Nordstrom." He kept that name ever since, and when he joined the navy it caused some confusion because his birth certificate had a different name.

Life was fun down on the "farm" but there were a lot of chores, and on Saturday our job was to cut a large area of lawn in the morning. This took some time and we were usually still working when all the neighborhood kids had already started to play. Since that time, gardening was never a favorite pastime of mine or my brothers.

Like most children, we thought our mother was the best person in the world. She was always very loving and supportive of her family, and felt that she could never do too much for her children. If she thought we were too thin, which was most of the time, she would fill us with rich foods. Even our milk was so creamy it was more like half-and-half. When we were quite young, we didn't like milk, so mother used to give us ten cents for every glass we drank. After a while, we began to like drinking milk so much, that mother was able to lower the price until we were drinking it for free.

In 1916 we moved to a house in Montlake. Father wanted us to go to the University, and this way it would be a lot closer. It became the family home for many years. The three boys still slept out on a sleeping porch that was covered but open on the sides, even during the coldest winter nights.

They were still working on the Montlake Canal when we moved there. At the time, it was just an old logging canal. In the winter it would freeze over and we would ice skate on it. The bridge wasn't built then, but down where the Seattle Yacht Club is now, there was a fellow who operated sort of a neighborhood ferry. From seven in the morning until five in the afternoon he would take you across in his rowboat for ten cents. I can still recall running like mad to catch the last ferry, because if you missed it, you had to walk all the way back to the University District and across the University Bridge. I made that walk many times.

Later on, when we attended the University, mother would sometimes wake up and find a house full of fraternity brothers who had spent the night. It meant more work for her, but she always made them feel welcome. She just loaded down the table with extra plates and made eveyone eat a hearty breakfast. Maybe she thought some of them were too thin, too.

One of my biggest joys in growing up began in 1910 when my father purchased waterfront property on Hood Canal with a group of friends. This became our home during summer vacations.

My father would load us into a seven passenger Stoddard-Dayton touring car, complete with gas headlights. Our first planned stop would be at Camp Lewis, now Fort Lewis, where we would have lunch under the trees. I call it our first planned stop, because invariably along the way we would have to deal with two or three blowouts.

Tires weren't as reliable then as they are now, and fixing a flat was a tedious process. First the tire had to be removed from the wheel, which was difficult because tires didn't have mounted rims then. Next, the inner tube was repaired with a kit. Then the inner tube had to be put back on the wheel and pumped up by hand, a matter of plenty of elbow grease since tires carried eighty pounds of pressure each. So our drive would usually start early in the morning and end about 6:00 in the evening.

Once there, we tended to stay for the entire summer. My father would take a steamer that ran from Union City to Seattle and go back to mind the store for one week, and then return to the Canal for a week. He and his partner, Mr. Wallin, took turns doing this.

We lived in tents on frame floors, with no running water and a little cook stove. We had a clay tennis court even before a permanent house, but it wasn't much of a court as you can imagine. There was also swimming and boating, and we would hike the Olympic Mountains with friends our own age. Often we would drag underbrush to the beach and build huge bonfires as the sun went down.

My father called it "pioneering," and even though he had done plenty of that in his life, he continued to spend summers there with his family for thirty years because mother wanted it so. "It's good for the children," she said.

I couldn't have agreed with her more.

*Front—father, mother and my sister Esther.*
*Back row—Everett, Libby, Illsley, Lloyd, Kitty and me.*

# Life with Father

I can't say enough about my father. He was a wonderful man. He always like to keep busy and stayed in good health until just before his death in 1963.

Through his example we learned to believe in ourselves and the idea that success can be achieved with hard work. He arrived in this country in 1887, a fifteen-year-old Swedish immigrant who couldn't speak a word of English, with a bankroll of $5. He worked his way across the country with a series of back-breaking, dangerous jobs, with one adventure following another.

One day he happened to go into Arlington, a town north of Seattle. At breakfast he picked up a newspaper, and there he saw front page news that would change his life.

11

Gold had been discovered in Alaska. So he joined the thousands of eager hopeful men who journeyed north to the freezing Klondike. There, unlike many others, he eventually did strike gold, enough to return to Seattle and open a business with Carl F. Wallin. They called it Wallin & Nordstrom and began selling shoes at their store on Fourth and Pike in 1901.

My father had a partner in Alaska who would do anything my father wanted him to. He was brave and strong, and could pull a sled twenty miles along the frozen river to Dawson for supplies. His name was Yukon and he was a huge St. Bernard that stood two inches above our dining room table. When father left Alaska, a lot of people wanted to buy Yukon, but father wouldn't part with him.

When father returned to Seattle he renewed his acquaintance with Hilda Carlson, another Swedish immigrant. They were married and moved into a house close to town on Bellevue Street. Mother had to go shopping one day, and decided to walk down to the Bon Marche with Yukon. Before going inside, she told the dog to sit at the door and wait for her.

She got so busy that she left from another exit and forgot all about Yukon. When it was closing time, the people from the store went to lock the doors, but they couldn't come out to lock Yukon's door because every time they did, he growled at them and wouldn't allow it. Finally, someone got close enough to read the name tag, saw Nordstrom on it, and walked across the street to fetch my father.

Yukon wasn't mean, he was just a good watchdog. Mother said that when we were kids she never worried about us playing in the front yard. If we stepped onto the sidewalk, Yukon would push us back into the yard. He was also smart. According to father, you could talk to this dog and he would understand you. I don't know about that, but I remember he was smart enough to know all the butcher shops and made his daily rounds.

Before going to Alaska, father worked in logging camps

up and down the coast. He often worked as a "faller," which carried a lot of responsibility since the trees had to fall in just the right place or there could be trouble. There were plenty of trees to be felled at our summer place on Hood Canal, and when I was young I spent a good deal of time with him on the other end of a saw. Our neighbors would occasionally ask him to help clear the larger trees off their land. One of his favorite tricks was to place a stake a few yards away and cut the tree so it would fall and drive the stake into the ground. He rarely missed.

My father was good with an ax, but he was never a particularly good driver. For example, he never could adjust to using turn signals. He would simply lower the driver's window about two inches and stick his finger out in the rain. As he got older he was involved in a few minor accidents, nothing really serious, but once his housekeeper was jarred a bit. That time the insurance company called us. The agent, whom we knew well, told us, "Your father is getting on in years now, and perhaps he should not be driving these days."

We agreed, but presenting our case to father was difficult, because he truly enjoyed driving. However, a friend of father's, one of our older shoe clerks, was retired and a widower like father. We talked with him, then approached father with an idea.

"You're getting older now," we said, "and you're starting to have a few accidents. Maybe you deserve to have someone doing your driving for you. Fred Bulger is in a position to drive you around town whenever you wish, so why not have him be your driver?"

Naturally, this hurt his feelings a bit and he replied, "Let me think it over." The next day he came to us and said, "I have decided to give up driving and so I asked Fred Bulger to move in with me and do the driving. However, I am making this decision not because of my accidents, but because of a situation I created for myself that is a bit troublesome. Since mother passed away, I've been seeing quite a few widows. Whenever there is a party I spend great

13

deal of time picking them up and driving them all home. And that's just too much work!''

Father always enjoyed coming to the store after he retired. He would sit in the men's department usually and his old friends would come in to visit him. We furnished an office for him upstairs where he and his friends would go to play cards or cribbage.

He continued coming in until he was over 90 years old. Sometimes he would walk around and look like a clerk. More than once a customer commented, ''I know these Nordstrom boys are loyal to their employees, but I can't understand why they keep working that old man. They really should retire him.''

When father was in his seventies the family threw a big birthday party for him at the Washington Athletic Club. Many of his old friends came. One of them brought a gift from the Alaska gold rush days. It was a full length bear skin coat with a high collar, but a pretty sorry specimen, all dirty and worn out with smooth spots. My father though, put it right on. Then he drew himself up, put his hands out in front as if driving a dog sled and shouted, ''Mush! Mush!'' much to everyone's delight.

We had a special surprise prepared for father that day. Days earlier we had arranged for *The Seattle Times* to stop its presses for a moment and insert a new headline on the front page of their regular edition. So just as we were having drinks before dinner, in came a newspaperboy shouting the day's top story, ''Extra! Extra! Nordstrom has a birthday.'' This time it was father's turn to be delighted.

That's what life with father was like. Though he lived to be 93, he never became crotchety and stubborn as many men do. He loved life and he lived it to the fullest.

# Business as a Boy

B Y the time my brother and I started in the shoe business, Wallin & Nordstrom had moved to a new location on Second between Pike and Union. I was about twelve when I started going in on Saturdays with my father. From our home in Rainier Valley, we would walk a half mile, then take a streetcar to the store. For lunch, father would take us to his favorite haunt, Hallberg's on Pike Street, which was a big treat because it made us feel so grown-up.

My first job was as a "button-boy." In those days women wore high button shoes and to achieve a good fit, the buttons usually had to be adjusted for each customer. The clerk would mark the new positions for the buttons with a pencil, then hand them to one of the button boys. On busy days

15

there were as many as three of us in the back adjusting buttons while the customers waited for their shoes. We cut the buttons off by hand, then used a machine with a foot stamp to reposition them.

After a while I started doing more stock work, which was fun, because I got to push tall ladders around and scamper up and down them. The store had a twenty-foot ceiling, and in those days we had an office up front on a balcony. To complete a sale, you would put the shoes and money in a basket, then yank on a rope to send it up to the office where it was rung up and wrapped. Then you would yank on another rope and it would come back down. Most of the stores had similar systems, and one day my future mother-in-law was shopping at the Bon, when one of those baskets came down and hit her on the nose.

I also helped with deliveries. In the evenings I would take packages through the alley exit, cross Union and then take another alley between Second and Third to the tiny office of United Parcel Service. Now they're a nationwide delivery service, but at the time they were a small Seattle company started by the Casey family with a couple of trucks and a few motorcycles. They only made deliveries in the city, and we were one of their first accounts.

We worked all the way through school, but that didn't keep us from pursuing other interests. Everett was the best student and the most consistently occupied with the business at an early age. He knew from the start that he wanted to be in the shoe business. He liked sports, but he was so small as a student at Franklin High School, he played on the midget teams. He was only 16 when he graduated and was still wearing short pants when he entered college. It's only fair to add that he eventually grew to over six feet tall and became a great golfer.

Lloyd, the youngest, had a terrific personality and was student body president of Broadway High School. We all liked sports, but Lloyd was the most athletic. He played basketball but really excelled at tennis. He became the

Northwest intercollegiate tennis champion, played at Forest Hills and was invited to play on the U.S. Davis Cup Team.

Baseball, football, tennis—I loved them all. I was playing center on the basketball team at Broadway, the tallest man on the team as a sophomore, trying to work my way up to the first squad, when the blow fell.

We had to be checked over by the school doctor and I went with the rest of the team. He was examining me when he said, "Son, who's your family doctor? You go see him right away." I went to see our doctor and then was sent to see a specialist. The verdict was that I had an "athletic heart" twice the size of a normal heart. For a while, they weren't even going to let me go to school, let alone play sports. But I prevailed upon them to let me go to school, if I took it easy. And that's what I did, on doctor's orders, all the way through high school and college. After being athletic and all, well, it was hard to take.

Luckily, I had another interest, one that I shared with my father. We both liked automobiles. And unlike either of my brothers, I happened to be mechanically inclined.

I was driving by the time I was thirteen. A license was not required in those days, all you needed was the ability to drive well enough so as not to be a nuisance. On Sunday mornings I would join my father and work on the family car. After I spent some time washing it, he would let me drive it around the block.

When I was sixteen, my father ordered a special Premier automobile. The local dealer told him that there was only one car of this kind around, and that it was in Spokane. He offered to have it sent over, but father had a better idea, "I'll send my son Elmer for it. That way I know it will arrive in good shape."

So I went to Spokane and made plans to leave with the car at about 6:00 in the evening. But before I left, I happened to meet a salesman for the company who asked if he could come along with me to Seattle, and I agreed to take him. Now, when I said goodbye to father, he told me not to drive his new car over twenty miles an hour, and I dutifully kept to that speed the entire trip. It took us eighteen hours. Occasionally the salesman would say, "Looks like the road is clear ahead, you can speed up now." But each time I had to remind the poor fellow that I had strict orders.

*Shoes displayed in the windows of the University store, 1925.*

# The University Years

WALLIN & Nordstrom opened their second store, the University store, in 1923. Everett, who had just graduated from the U of W Business School at age 20, was in charge of the opening. He managed the store for some years, then later I ran it and finally Lloyd ran it. So all three of us managed it at one time or another.

When I was at the University, I used to drive the Wallin & Nordstrom company truck to transfer stock from downtown to the University store. I would make the trip almost every day. This truck was actually an old Model T that had been converted into a covered panel carrier.

Whenever there was a snowfall, there would be a terrific rush of people wanting galoshes. So I would excuse myself from school and come in to work the sales floor or drive downtown to collect more stock. I remember one winter in particular, when I had to drive the truck downtown more than once through the snow to pick up a load of new style galoshes that had just appeared on the scene, called "Zippers." They were a hot item for cold days.

The University store stayed open until 9:00 on Christmas Eve for the last minute shoppers. And since the day after Christmas was usually one of the busiest of the year, we would often work until midnight on Christmas Eve and part of Christmas day. It was a lot of work, but that's "shoe biz," so to speak.

We didn't have a janitor in those days. Every morning we would get in early to vacuum the carpets and wash the outside of the windows. Once in a while we would trim the windows, which meant taking out all the shoes, washing the windows, then trying to rearrange the shoes in an interesting fashion.

All three brothers went to the University of Washington, we all graduated from the business school and we all joined the Beta fraternity. Everett joined first, but initially pledged a different fraternity. My older sister, who didn't really approve of his choice, sicked some of her friends on him and got him to change his mind. Those were the days of Prohibition and college people never drank, quite a change from now. Anybody who came to a fraternity dance with liquor on his breath was kicked out.

There was one night while I was in college that I'll never forget. It was a big party to celebrate the opening of the Olympic Hotel, the grandest hotel in town, and since it was built as a community enterprise, much of the city was involved in the festivities.

I went with a friend of mine and our dates. Opening night was a black-tie affair and cost $10 a plate, which was a lot of money at the time. My father heard about the cost and thought it was outrageous, so he didn't go. But I could not miss this event.

There were different orchestras in each of the hotel's dining rooms, and we danced in one room or the other the whole evening. We were seated for dinner in the Venetian Room and I can point out where the four of us sat to this day. It was wonderfully exciting and when we finally left at 3:00 in the morning, the party was still going strong. It was an evening Seattle talked about for years.

In 1923 when I was just starting college, my father took us on a trip to Alaska. He was interested in retracing the route he had taken twenty-five years earlier when he joined the Klondike Gold Rush. This trip was a major event for me, because back then people didn't travel very much. Everett, who had been to Alaska twice before to work in the canneries during summer vacations, remained behind to manage the newly opened University store. My sister, Esther, was married by then and didn't accompany us either. So mother, father, Lloyd and I made the trip.

We sailed on a steamer to Skagway and crossed White Pass to Whitehorse just as my father had during the gold rush, only this time instead of hauling hundreds of pounds of gear up that steep, frozen grade, we rode in comfort on the narrow gauge White Pass & Yukon Railroad.

The Alcan Highway wasn't constructed yet. In fact, there were no roads at all to the Klondike, so we booked passage on a river boat, a wood-burning paddlewheeler, that took us down the mighty Yukon River. Many times we pulled into shore to load fuel that had been cut and stacked by the local residents during the cold and dark winters.

We were the first boat through that summer after the break up of the winter ice, and we were carrying mail and supplies to the people up there for the first time since the previous fall. They would come running to meet us, alerted by their dogs, which announced our arrival with furious barking.

The trip took eight full days. I remember how difficult it was to sleep since the nights were never completely dark. By the time we reached Circle City, aptly named since it was just inside the Arctic Circle, it was light for 24 hours.

The trip was made even more interesting because the water was very low. At times, crewmen had to precede the boat in a skiff, prodding with an oar to search for deep water. Once, while navigating Lake LeBarge, the silt was so thick that the captain had to turn the boat around with the big paddlewheel up front to get us through. We would sit in the stern and watch the boat hit these river mud hills, then feel it as we rode up, over and down again.

Finally we landed at Dawson, and from there traveled up to the Klondike to find my father's old land claim. After all the anticipation we arrived at the creek that father had worked so hard and so long at panning for gold, and it was just a bunch of huge rock piles. A major mining company had used mammoth dredges on the site. Still, that was where father struck gold, and where he might have become a rich man, except for an interesting story he tells in his book.

As he tells it, there was a lot of jostling for claim sites during the Gold Rush and some dubious frontier justice. After he found gold, a man decided to dispute his claim, even though father had a right to the site and had worked it for two years. But the man had the upper hand — his brother was the local Land Commissioner. So his friends advised father that he had a choice: he could sell out for something, or hold out and get nothing.

My father took their advice. He knew that especially in that rugged outpost, getting out with a little something was better than being stuck with a lot of nothing.

*Everett and me the year after I graduated from college.*

# Leaving the Nest

AFTER college a lot of young people want to get out on their own and try something new. In Everett's case, after receiving his degree he managed the University store for several years, then left to become the West Coast representative for the J.P. Smith Shoe Company.

By the time I graduated in 1926 I was pretty serious about getting into the shoe business. However, I assumed that it would be helpful to receive some outside experience in the industry. We were acquainted with a Mr. Gibbs, the senior merchandising manager at Marshall Field's in Chicago. Through him I was able to secure a position, and worked in one department after another for about a year, learning on several levels how a major store merchandised and sold shoes.

At the end of that time, when I returned to Seattle, my father asked me what I had learned. "In all honesty," I said, "I did not bring back a lot of good ideas about what I should be doing in the retail business. But I certainly learned several things I should not do."

"In that case," my father said, "you learned quite a bit."

Selling shoes in Chicago was a good experience. I was on my own, seeing a lot of new things and meeting new people. I particularly remember meeting a girl who was going out with one of the men in the shoe department. She was an elevator operator at Marshall Field's who later on made movies "on the road" with Bob Hope and Bing Crosby. Her name was Dorothy Lamour.

Chicago has always been a good city for sports, and this was true when I was there. USC had a very strong football team that year and they were scheduled to play the perennial champions, Notre Dame, at Soldier Field. The problem was, they played on Saturday and I was scheduled to work. It was going to be too good to miss. So at lunchtime, I punched out and ran the twelve blocks to the stadium. In order to see more of the game, I asked a friend at the store to punch me back in at the proper time, which he did. The game was even better than expected, and it wasn't until the end of the third quarter that my guilty conscience won over my sports fever, and I ran back to the store. As it turned out, they never missed me.

Another sporting event I will never forget was also at Soldier Field. Gene Tunney and Jack Dempsey met in a match that became famous as "the long count fight." It was billed beforehand as the fight of the century, and even the cheap seats were $10. The friend I shared lodgings with declined to go because of the expense, but I couldn't miss it.

When I arrived at the stadium, I found that my $10 seat was so far away from the action that you could barely see the ring. However, during the preliminary fights, someone cut the rope that divided us from the more expensive seats and all of us in the stands pushed down to fill the empty places in the closer sections. So when the main event started, I was in a $40 seat.

The fight was outstanding. During the fifth round, Dempsey knocked Tunney down with a solid blow. Dempsey was supposed to move immediately to a neutral corner before the referee could begin counting, but for some reason he hesitated a few important seconds. This gave Tunney the chance to recover before the count was finished, and after he got back up he fought all the harder.

We were supposed to be sitting on benches but the excitement was so great during the fight that everyone was standing on them and shouting. Occasionally someone in front of us would fall backwards off the bench and start a chain reaction of bodies falling back like tenpins. So while I watched the fight I also had to watch for the next wave of falling bodies in order to jump down off the bench and get out of harm's way.

Several fist fights broke out in the stands. It was a loud and raucous crowd, and there was plenty of drinking going on. This rowdiness all came to a head when the fight was over because unfortunately, no one could hear the ringmaster's announcement of the winner. Someone would say that Dempsey won, and another man would hit him. When someone else claimed Tunney was the winner, another fight would start.

I couldn't tell who won the real fight, but I decided to leave before I got stuck in the other ones. I jumped onto an elevated train that took me to the north part of the city where I lived. At my stop, I had to buy an "extra" that had been rushed to the newsstands, just to see who won.

About the time I was getting ready to leave Marshall Field's, I heard about an attractive position with General Motors. This interested me quite a bit because it would have involved working with a new line of cars, but the job didn't start until a couple of months later, and I was eager to return to Seattle. There was a business opportunity brewing that would set the course of my life.

25

*With all the signs, there was no mistaking our store on Second Avenue.*

# Buying the Business

WHEN my father sold the business to Everett and me we were both pretty young. I was 24, Everett was 26. My father's friends were concerned about this and mentioned it to him more than once. When they did, my father always answered, "I only went through the sixth grade in Sweden, but these boys are college graduates. I'm sure they'll do a better job than I did."

We bought out my father in 1928 and he retired. At first Mr. Wallin didn't want to sell his share, but after he saw how my father was living and enjoying life, he changed his mind and sold out the following year.

Right away we discovered the joy of owning our own business. About a month after we purchased the company, we came in one morning and discovered that professionals had broken through the ceiling at night, blown open the safe and made off with all the receipts. There had been close to $8,000 in the safe, but our insurance only covered losses of up to $1,000. So it was a $7,000 lesson, learned the hard way.

Even though we owned the business, it was all on paper. Neither of us had any up-front capital, so father extended a loan to us and even co-signed a bank note so we could have some working capital.

With the money we borrowed, we improved and expanded the Second Avenue store. We leased the space next to us and doubled the square footage in our new store. We modernized the interior, removed the baskets that were used to carry money and purchases up to the cashier on the mezzanine, rearranged the shelves so that we didn't have to go up and down long ladders, and made the sales floor more comfortable. We also put in a balcony for offices and created a basement area for lower priced merchandise. In all, we fashioned a store that was considered very modern.

At that time the store had a reputation for quality, conservative shoes. We carried very little high fashion, instead, we concentrated on the "health" shoes that were very popular. When we finished work on the new, enlarged store we had a grand opening and there were long lines outside the store all day because of a man named Dr. Locke.

Dr. Locke was gaining national publicity as a foot specialist who could cure problem feet with a few simple adjustments. We had one of his representatives at our opening and people came in droves to have their feet worked on by him. Many claimed that he helped them a great deal. It certainly helped our business. Years later I had a chance to see Dr. Locke himself in action. He sat in the middle of a circle of chairs occupied by people who would hold up their feet as he swung around on his own chair with wheels. After manipulating someone's feet for a minute or so, he would be handed a dollar bill which he would pocket before swinging over to the next customer. In the meantime, someone else would take the chair just vacated and wait his or her turn. I never tried it myself, but I saw a lot of smiles on people walking away from these adjustments.

Shortly after buying the business we were in for another shock, and unlike being robbed, it was something we couldn't have protected ourselves against. It came with Black Tuesday and was called The Great Depression.

Although it took a bit longer to reach Seattle, it brought a very grim picture when it arrived. The financial scene was at its most critical point in history, and we had just assumed sizable debts and a retail business that would now have to endure some very difficult times.

From the beginning of this venture we agreed that if ever father's interests were jeopardized, we would liquidate our holdings and save him from any loss. My father was not a wealthy man and most of his net worth was in this business. So if we went under, he would have gone down with us. Business got worse and worse, and it looked like we would lose everything. But with liquidation staring us in the face, we had an encouraging upturn and business improved. That was as close as we came to selling out.

When Lloyd graduated from college in 1933, it was time for him to come on board as planned. By this time Everett and I had put five years into the business, and Lloyd wanted to pay his part before coming in. He didn't want to join for free. "You're not making enough money for yourselves as it is," he said. So we asked our accountant to compute our net worth in order to determine how much to charge Lloyd for his one-third interest. We assumed we had built up a bit of equity. After a few days, our accountant came back to us with his figures. "You have no net worth," he explained. So Lloyd joined the team with only his obligation to work hard and help us meet our payments.

Despite the Depression, we managed to meet every bank payment on time and continued to pay off father's loan, except for one period when we had to delay his installments for a few months.

Years later when we finally finished paying our debt to father, he shook each of our hands and told us, "This is the only investment I made during those years that I didn't lose money on."

*The team—Lloyd, Everett and me, together with our father in later years.*

# The Team

WE had our share of troubles during the Depression, which I'll cover in the next chapter, but we had something going for us, something that helped us weather the storm. It was our team: Everett, Lloyd and me. Any success we had was the result of all our efforts.

We shared our work evenly and each of us worked as hard as we could. As time went on we divided the responsibilities into areas. Lloyd and Everett merchandised women's shoes, the bulk of our business. I merchandised men's and children's shoes.

Everett was good with figures and a very sound financial man. Lloyd was articulate and personable, a man who performed well in the public eye, and he was in charge of all our publicity. I handled union negotiations and, being mechanically inclined, supervised store operations.

I have to confess that we were all a bit retiring and weren't particularly strong salesman. In fact, others could sell rings around us. We weren't the best by a long shot. Even so, we were all out there on the floor selling shoes when we could. On busy days one of us would watch the floor and the other two would be selling. But we didn't necessarily run a high book.

There was a good spirit of competition among the three of us. Each of us merchandised our own particular areas and we all knew how each area was doing. So if one brother was doing better than the others, it was apparent to all. We had no prizes, and we didn't boast about it, but we always knew which brother was doing the best. Knowing it only made the other two try harder.

I can say with all honesty that we got along very well with one another. We realized at the beginning that our ability to work well together was crucial to the success of our business. Even though we were working together in an office so small our desks were side by side, we kept our heads and moved quickly to resolve any differences.

Whenever a subject came up that would affect the business as a whole, we discussed options and weighed consequences as a team. Very rarely was there any disagreement. When there was, we would resolve the matter with a vote, and the majority would rule. Luckily there were seldom any actual votes. It usually ended up all for one and one for all.

Being in business with two brothers had its advantages. For example, we made it a practice to have one of us in the store at all times, so if you had to leave, you knew the business was in good hands. But I suppose it had its disadvantage as well. It was kind of like being married—you worked together for a common goal, but you didn't get your own way all the time.

Speaking of being married, there were other members of the team who made contributions time and time again.

These were our wives, and later on our families, who backed us up "for better or for worse" and managed to help keep things on an even keel. I remember more than one Christmas Eve when my brothers and I would duck out of the store to buy gifts for our wives, making sure we spent around the same amount of money, since at times there wasn't a lot to go around.

Chances are, if I had been alone in this business, I might have drawn a bit more out of the business when we became more successful and had more capital. I might not have spent as much time at work as I did.

It's very possible my brothers felt this way, too. Who knows, maybe if one of us had come up to the other two and said, "We're doing well now, let's take it a little easier," we might have said, "Great idea!" But none of us did.

We wanted to be successful. We wanted to be the best that we could.

It wasn't until we incorporated in 1938 that titles became a legal requirement. Up until then we were a partnership, and these formalities weren't necessary.

Everett seemed like a natural choice for president. As the oldest brother, Lloyd and I looked up to him. He was an extremely level-headed man, constantly exuding those qualities that can be defined as genuine leadership. Once an earthquake rocked the store with a series of shocks that toppled displays and everyone started to panic. Then they saw Everett standing by the elevator with his arms folded, a calming smile on his face.

He was always athletic and had a tremendous interest in sports. An admitted "statistics nut," he brought obscure but interesting figures to our frequent conversations about sports. He knew the value of teamwork and thrived in a competitive environment. His wife, Libby, noted that he would come home more tired on slow days than busy days, and that he seldom got angry or swore, "except on the golf course ."

Everett was also a stickler for quality. At one time we

had women's pumps in stock that were causing a problem. It seemed that the uppers were separating from the soles near the ball of the foot, so Everett called the manufacturer about it. They told him, "They're not all bad. Just send back the ones that come apart." My brother's response was to sit in the stock room, taking every pair of shoes and popping them apart. He could do it easily with his thumb and he popped them by the hour, just to make sure that no customer would have a problem.

When we approached Everett about becoming president he gave it some serious thought. He knew that in many companies, the oldest brother became president and remained president, relegating the younger brothers to positions down the line. But Everett insisted on a different plan. "I'll agree to be president for now," he said, "but only if we agree to rotate the titles."

And so we did. We would work our way up to president, then drop down to secretary/treasurer for two years. Then we would serve as vice-president for two years, until we became president again.

Occasionally people would ask us our titles and we sometimes had trouble remembering who was who on that day. We had to know when signing papers, but that's the only time the members of the team needed a title.

*Seattle's Hooverville during the Depression. Photo courtesy of the Museum of History and Industry.*

# The Depression

D URING the worst of the Depression it seemed as if no one had any money. The entire country was forced to come to terms with the value of a single penny. Back yard vegetable gardens appeared, and walks in the park replaced pastimes that cost money.

Our sales were way down and retail prices began to fall lower and lower. Wholesale prices fell, too. Shoes we paid $10 for we could now buy for $8. But if we had 3,000 pairs of those shoes in stock, we lost $6,000.

Customers held on to what little money they had. They were watching the prices fall and thinking, "If I can get another month out of the shoes I have now, the price of new ones will be lower still." And they were right. We had to sell twice as many shoes just to break even.

The situation demanded hard work. We put in long hours, watched our overhead carefully, controlled our buying and markdowns, personally attended to every minor detail and worked closely on all matters. Our main concern was to pay for our store and achieve a solid footing. And we found that, with our combined efforts, we could make ends meet. We got by.

I remember a night out in those days. It was a fancy dinner/dance in the Georgian Room of the Olympic Hotel. We enjoyed a fine steak dinner and danced for much of the night to a large band. The cost for the entire evening's entertainment was a dollar and fifty cents—quite a change from a similar evening back in the "Roaring Twenties."

At the onset of the Depression, banks all across the country began to fail. Everyone was hearing stories of people being completely wiped out or retaining only twenty-five cents on the dollar when their bank folded. And fold they did, even banks that had been in business for fifty years. This prompted the infamous "Run on Banks" that threatened the entire nation's economy until the federal government stepped in.

The Run on Banks happened quite rapidly and reached a peak on a Monday. I remember the day well because I had to draw out money from our University bank and deposit it in our downtown bank as a normal business procedure.

That morning I arrived at the University store about 7:30, and noticed that people were already lining up outside the bank, waiting to draw their money out. We used the National Bank of Commerce, and every day we would deposit the receipts from the University store until we had accumulated a few thousand dollars. Then we would withdraw the funds and transfer them downtown where all the bills were paid by our bookkeeper.

At this time we had quite a bit of money in the bank, maybe eight or nine thousand dollars. We usually withdrew it when it was much less than that. The situation didn't look good, and I began to worry that our assets could be frozen or even lost completely if the bank collapsed.

I called Everett downtown and asked him what he thought. He told me there were long lines downtown as well. I asked, "How much do we have in your account?" He replied, "We have very little and we're writing checks." So I asked him, "What do you think we should do?" He answered, "Well, I just don't know." So I waited.

The manager of the University bank was a good friend of mine and I hated like the devil to go in there, because if I was going to draw our money out I would have to walk right by his desk.

All morning the lines just got longer and finally, around noon, I reached my limit of endurance. I got in line. When I drew out our money I received it in thousand dollar bills. Naturally I was concerned with carrying that much cash around, so I decided to put it in our safety deposit box in the bank's basement, where I could pick it up later.

I didn't get back to the bank that day and the very next day, March 22, the federal government declared the "Bank Holiday" that closed all the financial institutions in the country until economic solutions could be achieved. So even though our funds were safe, I couldn't get in to get them. I was trumped no matter how I played it. When the banks reopened a few days later, I gathered the money and rather sheepishly took it downtown to make a deposit.

Back in 1929 just before Black Tuesday, I had been talking with that same bank manager when he suggested I buy some stock in the National Bank of Commerce. "We're doing well," he claimed, "and you can buy the stock on an installment plan." Persuaded, I purchased twenty shares at $46, with a total investment of $920 and a year to pay for them. Then came the stock market crash and stocks went down across the board, including mine.

After the crash, I approached my friend the banker and explained not too happily that I was paying on a $700 note for stocks that were now worth $500. His response was,

"You have the right to cancel your debt and give up your stocks if you choose. Just forget about the money you have put in and you can bow out with no hard feelings." But that didn't sound right to me and I continued to scrape together the money to pay for them. I still have those stocks in my portfolio today, and I have a feeling that they turned out to be a rather good investment. The National Bank of Commerce eventually became Rainier Bank, and the stock has split quite a few times.

That wasn't my first venture in stocks. I had a school friend whose father was interested in gold mines and I spent a couple of hundred dollars losing money on his prospecting schemes.

An early shot of our "risky" new location at 5th and Pike.

# Making the Best of Things

THOSE were rough times to be in business, but not everything about the Depression years was bad. In fact, we made some decisions that turned out to be very good. After all, just because you're broke doesn't mean you can't fall in love and get married.

Lloyd was first to step up to the altar. He and Illsley tied the knot in 1932. The following year matrimony caught up with Everett, and he and Libby joined their lives together.

I met Kitty, my wife-to-be, at our summer place on Hood Canal. Her family also had a summer place up there, and at first she was Lloyd's friend since they were the same age.

We were married in 1934 and traveled to Chicago to see

the World's Fair. Chevrolets were being manufactured there at the time and we bought one, then drove up to Milwaukee to visit Kitty's relatives.

Milwaukee was home of the Nunn-Bush shoe factory and we spent a day viewing the operations and visiting with Mr. Nunn and Mr. Bush, whom I met for the first time. From there we drove on to Ontario, Canada, and New York City where we stayed for five or six days. It was a typical Nordstrom honeymoon, going into every shoe store in the city. Just talk with any of our wives and you'll hear that they spent a lot of time traipsing behind us looking at shoes.

By 1935 business had picked up a little, enough so that Kitty and I were thinking of buying our first house. We figured we could afford to spend $5,000 maximum. Nonetheless, one day we peeked at a fine place on Capitol Hill for $9,000. The owners had just put $2,000 worth of work into it, and the real estate agent encouraged us to make an offer since they were desperate to sell. So we made an offer that we thought they might consider a joke, since it was so low. We said we might be able to afford $7,000.

Two weeks went by and we were relieved that we had not heard back from the agent. Then one day he called and said, "It's yours." We both panicked because we had no idea how we were going to meet the payments. But somehow we managed and lived there for the next ten years.

In 1937 Everett, Lloyd and I made a major decision, one that started out because of a big mistake.

The lease on our Second Avenue store was expiring on the first of that year. We should have negotiated a new lease during Christmas time, but that's a busy time for retailers, and immediately after the holiday itself there are sales and exchanges, and then inventory work required for the new year statements. We were so busy, we failed to exercise our option for renewal when the lease ran out.

It was close to the end of January when we wrote a letter stating our wish to remain in the store for another five years. That's when we received a big surprise. Our landlord wrote back with a strongly worded statement that we missed our deadline and no longer had our option. So we met with him and discovered that he intended to raise our rent considerably. He thought he had us over a barrel.

It was obvious that this landlord was capable of taking an unfair advantage when he could, so we started looking around for another location. Eventually we found that the Owl Drugstore on Fifth Avenue between Pike and Pine was available. We signed a lease and opened our new store in December.

Everyone thought this move was risky business, and in fact it was. At the time, Second Avenue was a busy shopping area and we were doing well there. The new location was on the outskirts of the downtown business area. Our father, who had not involved himself with the business from the day we bought it, made an attempt to prevent us from making an unnecessary and potentially disastrous move. Our old landlord heard that we were serious about moving and offered us a renewal on the original terms.

However, my brothers and I viewed our move as a challenge. Taking calculated chances in business is the best way to grow and succeed. We were leaving a good location to seize an opportunity to grow faster. And as it turned out, we did.

Our new landlord remained on excellent terms with us and he was very supportive of our desire to expand. Whenever adjoining space became available, we were allowed first right of refusal and we always accepted more space. In stages over the next few years we expanded outwards and upwards, until we occupied all of the Ranke building.

It was at this location in 1959, not far from the first little Wallin & Nordstrom shoe store, that Nordstrom came to be known as the largest independently owned shoe store in the United States. Today, the location that was considered "out in the boondocks" when we moved there, is at the center of the downtown Seattle retail core, and serves as the corporate headquarters for our entire organization.

It all turned out for the best.

# Pearl Harbor Day

ON the morning of December 7, 1941, my wife Kitty and I were packing the car for a trip to Portland. By this time the Fifth Avenue and University stores were going strong and we had accumulated enough capital for expansion into other areas. Portland was the next largest city in the Pacific Northwest, and we had made up our minds to go down there. We were just waiting for the right opportunity.

That opportunity came when Bill Knight told us of his intention to retire and offered to sell us his store, the Knight Shoe Company. It was decided that one of the brothers should travel to Portland to talk with Mr. Knight, and I was selected.

As we packed for our trip, a neighbor strolled over with an odd look on his face. He had just heard some incredible news on the radio—Pearl Harbor had been attacked by the Japanese!

We were stunned. There were wars going on all over the world, but so far America had managed to stay out of them. Now we were involved, or were we? The early reports were very sketchy. Pearl Harbor still seemed a long way away and it was hard to realize the full seriousness of this tragic event. There was nothing to do, really, but go on with our trip.

By the time we got to the Cowlitz River, the National Guard was patrolling the bridges. We thought that was very unusual, of course. And when we arrived in Portland, we heard the whole story. We stayed up with friends until 3:00 in the morning listening to reports.

The next day I called Bill Knight and said, "We certainly can't talk now. There's too much going on." Then Kitty and I got in the car and headed back to Seattle.

On the way home there were even more soldiers on the bridges, and when we finally arrived in Seattle we found that a blackout was being enforced. We were lucky to make it home before dark, otherwise the soldiers would have stopped us. Even driving at night with your lights on was prohibited.

People today who didn't live through that experience may have a difficult time imagining what it was like in Seattle immediately after Pearl Harbor. No one knew what had happened to the huge Japanese fleet that had rained such complete destruction on our military base in Hawaii. All sorts of rumors went around that the Japanese were on their way to the West Coast. Seattle, the closest major port to Japan, with our naval bases and Boeing, seemed like the perfect target. We braced for an air attack.

Air raid sirens went off constantly whenever there was even the the slightest possibility of an attack, and barrage balloons filled the sky. Complete blackouts were ordered and heavy curtains had to be hung over all windows at night to prevent any light from escaping. Boeing landscaped the entire roof of their manufacturing plant with roads, cars, trees and houses to make it look like a residential area from the air. It was like living under a state of siege.

Eventually, it was confirmed that the Japanese fleet had turned back in the Pacific and headed for their home bases instead of continuing the attack. It was only then that the officials canceled orders for nightly blackouts. But for the years after that, the city lived with the knowledge that it would be one of the first targets if the war went badly and the Japanese reached the West Coast.

# Volunteering for Duty

"THERE are three brothers in this family and I'm the youngest," Lloyd said. "That makes me the logical choice to do our part for the war effort. I'm going to join up."

Everett and I looked at him. There was no use arguing, it wouldn't have made any difference. We were all married with families, and so there wasn't much chance of being drafted, but he had made up his mind to enlist. Shortly afterwards, Lt. J.G. Nordstrom received his commission in the U.S. Navy.

He was stationed nearby on Whidbey Island, which wasn't a bad assignment. Lloyd didn't like it though. He wanted to make a bigger contribution and repeatedly requested duty on a fighting ship. At length he received orders to report to the "Princeton," a cruiser that was under

43

construction on the East Coast.

When he arrived in Philadelphia he found that his ship was at least six months from completion, so he sent for his family and waited. It was there, near the end of the war, that my father thought of writing his book.

About that time I had to go back east on a buying trip, and I encouraged my father to go with me to visit Lloyd and his family. Once there, Lloyd's wife Illsley convinced my father to write down his early experiences in order to preserve them for his grandchildren.

As soon as we returned to Seattle, father went right to work recording his memories in longhand. Illsley collected a few old photographs and the family had the book published for father's birthday.

We never intended to print many books, but we found that the cost of producing 500 was about the same as 50, so we opted for the higher figure. When we presented them to father, he thought the quantity was totally absurd. "Two dozen is all we can ever use," he said.

Since then, we've had to reprint it four times.

Back in Philadelphia, the "Princeton" was launched. Lloyd had one ride on it, up and down the Potomac, and then the war ended. We all had some good laughs over that in later years.

Meanwhile, I'd been fighting the battle of Puget Sound.

At the outset of the war, the Navy asked local boat owners to help out as volunteers in the Coast Guard Auxiliary. I had a ChrisCraft at the time, and I agreed to donate my boat and my time one day a week.

Of course, if you volunteer your days to the Navy, you're sure to pull an all-night detail, which was one of the jobs I got. There was a submarine net strung across the narrow part of the passage into Bremerton. During darkness, the Navy closed it and no ship could get through unless it was given clearance. Our assignment was to anchor outside the net with a ship-to-shore radio. Whenever a ship approached, we would sail out and contact them with a loudspeaker. Then we would radio back to shore and wait for them to say, "Permission to approach granted," and open up the net. Or they would deny permission and the ship would have to anchor in the Sound until morning.

I did this for a few years, taking every Tuesday off work, which meant Everett made a contribution to the war effort too, by covering for me.

It got pretty spooky out there at night. There was a blackout around the naval base so there were no lights, and even the lighthouses were dimmed. You couldn't sleep because it was often rough and choppy out there, and because we had a lot of ships limping in all night long for repairs. I remember one cruiser that came through with its whole bow blown off. It must have hit a mine, which didn't encourage me much when it came to one of my other jobs for the Navy.

There was a concern that the Japanese would slip in secretly and mine the Sound, so the Navy sent out minesweepers every morning to open a safe channel from Tacoma all the way to Neah Bay on the Olympic Peninsula. Our job was to follow the minesweepers.

Generally we followed two minesweepers, which dragged long lines that would explode any magnetic mines, and devices called "pigs" that went along the bottom to snap any anchored mines. The lines went out several hundred feet, but floated only a foot or two below the surface. The fishing boats didn't realize how far back these lines went, so we carried a big red flag on our mast and if any boats started to cross the wake of the minesweepers, we would run out and chase them away.

After six months of this duty, we tied up one day alongside a minesweeper to have lunch on board with the crew. One of them was a young man from Seattle whom I knew, and I saw the opportunity to ask a question that I had been pondering.

"What happens," I asked, "if you explode a mine when we're behind you?" "Don't worry," he replied, "if we do, you'll never know what hit you."

It wasn't what you'd call a comforting response. ♪

*The interior of our Downtown store as it looked in 1942.*

# The War Years

SHORTLY after war was declared, prices were frozen, and doing business took on an entirely new complexion. We could sell as many shoes as we could get. The trouble was getting them.

Everything was scarce in those days. Manufacturers were expected to reserve one-half of their production for the war effort. Retailers were given a cutoff date, after which all prices had to remain in effect for the war's duration. People were issued ration stamps for practically everything, including shoes. As a I recall, shoes were stamp #17.

Customers would turn in a stamp when they bought a pair of shoes, then we would deposit the stamps in the bank. When we ordered more shoes, we were required to write a

46

special check, promising the manufacturer an equal amount of stamps. Without the proper stamps, shoes couldn't be shipped or sold. Some people tried to get around the system, few succeeded.

The first book of ration stamps had an expiration date, after which the stamps were no good. On the day they expired we came into work and found long lines outside the store. We had so many customers that day it was like a stampede. We couldn't take care of them all. The next book didn't have an expiration date and that made our jobs easier.

Leather was so scarce because of military needs, that all civilian shoes had rubber soles, and wingtips—which require extra leather—weren't made at all. It was so hard to get shoes, that I remember one Christmas when a customer insisted on buying two right slippers because that was all we had in the style she wanted.

The trick then, came down to traveling around the country, trying to find shoes that we could sell. Traveling in those days was by trains, which were equipped with drawing rooms and private compartments, showers, club cars and smoking rooms. The trouble was, the trains were often either crowded or sold out, and since there was a lot of troop movement, your train could be sidetracked at any time.

I remember one trip in particular. My wife Kitty often accompanied me, and this time we were scheduled to go to Red Wing, Minnesota, where there was a shoe factory. We took the Milwaukee Road which let us off about midnight in this small town. The station was deserted except for one man and I asked him how to get a cab. "No cabs," he replied. "Well," I said, "where's the hotel?" "Four blocks up the hill," he told us. So Kitty and I picked up our bags and started climbing. It wasn't much of a town. It wasn't much of a hotel, either.

After finishing our business in Red Wing, we headed for Wausau, Wisconsin. We started on one train and then had to change to another train, a very crowded one. We looked around and there were no seats, except for one that

Kitty found in the ladies' room. It was a very popular one, though, and she had to keep getting up throughout the trip.

Finding shoes anywhere was an arduous task, but once in a while we got lucky. One time I found a broker in Chicago who was rumored to have access to a line of shoes. I approached him and he seemed a little reluctant, but I didn't want to take no for an answer. Eventually he said he could let me have 300. "Well, I don't want to seem ungrateful," I said, "but I sure could use more than 300 pairs." "300 pairs," he said, raising his eyebrows, "I'm talking about 300 dozen." "Oh," I said, "that's different."

We all made a lot of those buying trips, trying to find shoes. In the beginning, many shoes were manufactured in Massachusetts, but as labor costs went up back there, a number of factories moved to the St. Louis area. The high-quality, high-fashion shoes, however, remained in New York City.

One of the problems in getting there, or anywhere, was that it was almost impossible to get reservations. Fortunately I knew a freight agent along the way, who, for a $15 or $20 gratuity, would reserve seats.

Once we got where we were going, war regulations limited our stay in any one hotel to three days. When we had to stay longer than that, a few dollars across the counter would usually help extend our reservation. There was quite a bit of tipping under the table during the war. It was a way of life.

Shoe conventions were an excellent opportunity to see many lines in one place at a time, so we made it a practice to attend as many as we could. In most cases, two of us would go and one would remain behind to manage operations. Shoe manufacturers would reserve large sample rooms in great hotels like the Chicago Palmer House or the Stevens. Sometimes they would take over two or three floors. Then they would display their lines and stand around chatting with retailers from across the country.

I remember how Everett would view the samples. He

would walk slowly and silently around the room, every now and then stopping to inspect a pair in particular, then continue on with his hands behind his back. All the representatives waited breathlessly to answer his questions, but he rarely said a word. When he reached the door he would turn and thank them sincerely, then leave. He always made his decisions later, after he had gained an overview of the season's offerings.

At first, the manufacturers weren't that impressed with us. Seattle was the same as Podunk to them. But gradually they began to favor us because they could sense that we were a bit more aggressive and would probably be a good account after the war. Once I visited a small Italian manufacturer in Michigan who told me he couldn't possibly supply us with any house slippers, since his production was already allocated. I wrote him a check for several thousand dollars on the spot, and asked if it would make any difference. Prepaid orders were uncommon and he was delighted. We received a good shipment of men's house slippers shortly thereafter.

Being aggressive helped, but what also helped was building rapport with our suppliers and treating their representatives with common courtesy. For instance, we always believed that when a traveling salesman came to town, they should be entertained by us and not the other way around. We would pick up the tab in restaurants and quite often invited main-line salesmen to our homes for dinner. Our families reported that they looked forward to these dinner guests. The men usually had good personalities due to the nature of their jobs—a lot of them were selling air—and because they traveled so much, they usually had plenty of entertaining stories.

This rapport was very important during the war years, when shoes were hard to get. Often when a line of shoes became available, we were offered the right of first refusal. It also helped us with prompt deliveries, which were especially important because of our Seattle climate. Back east, fall shoes were not sold until September, but we needed them in

August. And we started our spring in February or March when there was still snow in other parts of the country.

Most shoe stores did a profitable business during the war because of the circumstances. There weren't as many shoes to sell, but there were never any markdowns, either. Unfortunately, these profitable times went to the heads of some store owners. They started buying bigger cars, taking extended vacations and generally living it up. I remember one store that closed early every day as soon as their selling quota was met.

After the war, when business decreased, these owners had a great deal of difficulty and some eventually lost their businesses. In fact, there were more shoe stores before the war, when Seattle was a much smaller city, than there are today.

On the other hand, we worked as hard as we could during those years. We wanted to build up our capital reserve so that we could expand when the opportunity arose. That opportunity was just around the corner.

# After the War

IN our early years in business, we were interested in expanding because it was apparent that we would need a larger base in order to support three growing families. We told ourselves, "The business will be big enough for all of us, or it will not be big enough for anyone."

From a business standpoint, there are many good reasons to expand. A commitment to growth affects the sales force. If you add new and bigger stores, your employees have more opportunities for advancement and promotion, and you can attract better people.

To help us get the experience we needed to grow, we joined some other retailers across the country just after the war, and formed a group called Shoes Associated.

There were twelve member stores at the time, representing Seattle, Denver, San Francisco and other cities in the east. Larger shoe stores have common problems and we thought by pooling our information we could help each other out.

We learned quite a bit in the beginning, but eventually we became the "bell cow" of the group. We were leading the way by being more aggressive, growing faster and coming up with most of the ideas. Some of the older stores were very set in their ways and couldn't change. At first we thought they were pretty cagey people because they had large stores, but as time went on we found that they weren't as cagey as we hoped they would be.

We were members for about 15 years and during that time our association had one distinct advantage. We all sent our sales figures to a common office and received ratings on how we were doing. This gave us an opportunity to pace ourselves with some of the largest shoe stores in the country, and instilled in us a sense of competition. Competition is always a driving force, and the competition we had in Seattle just wasn't that great.

In 1950 we were finally able to open our store in Portland. A good location became available on the corner of Southwest Broadway and Morrison and we moved in. The mayor of the city was there for our opening ceremonies, our friend Bill Knight ran a "welcome" ad, and our main competitor, Meier & Frank, advertised a half-price sale.

This was our first out-of-town venture. During the planning, my brothers and I discussed the best way to control operations. It was suggested that one of us relocate to Portland, but none of us wanted to leave Seattle. It's a wonderful city, the home office is here and this is where things happen. So we decided to try controlling operations from our home base, which has been our policy ever since.

Obviously it must have worked, as we eventually became the largest shoe store in Portland.

1950 also saw the opening of our first suburban store.

This was our first experience with a store in a shopping center, because Northgate was the first planned shopping center in the U.S.

The venture was viewed with a good deal of suspicion by most retailers since it was an entirely new concept. It would be fair to say that the leases did not go fast. Nonetheless, we were optimistic. Even so, we had no idea then just how good this store would turn out to be.

When we signed the lease at Northgate in 1949, I drove my father out to view the site of our new store. It was, in those days, quite a drive out in the country. It was raining when we got there. Construction had barely started and I pointed to a large mud hole, indicating that this was to be our new store. Father was absolutely floored and shook his head slowly. "I think that you are making a big mistake here," he said.

Actually, we had considered the venture very carefully. Everett had even chartered a light airplane to fly over the area and came back to report that there were large numbers of residential units going up in the immediate area. What seemed like an inordinately big risk to an older man such as my father was a challenging opportunity for us.

In later years we would discuss our increasingly fast growth with father. He would be frank with his opinions, but often added, "It does not seem logical to me that you should expand in this way, but the fact that I'm against it means that it will probably turn out well."

Today, I am the older man who advises caution when I comment on the decisions of the younger generation. But as I recently told a friend, "They do what they think is best anyway. That's why they are doing so well."

About the time we opened our Portland and Northgate stores, we also got involved with our first Leased Shoe Departments. This was another area of expansion that worked well for us for quite a number of years.

In Portland, Meier & Frank was tough competition for us and we reasoned that we could be more successful if we were able to control the shoe lines. If we were the only stores in town that carried a popular line of shoes, customers would naturally come to us.

However, since most manufacturers wanted to have their lines in both a shoe store and a department store within a city, it was impossible for us to carry an exclusive. So we approached the Portland department store of Olds & King and suggested that we lease their shoe department.

They were very receptive. As a general rule, department stores don't put a major emphasis on shoes because large inventories are required and the turnover is only twice or two and a half times a year at best. In comparison, apparel turns over much faster and requires far less capital investment.

Once we leased the shoe department at Olds & King, their parent company, Western Department Stores which later became a part of American Factors (AmFac), persuaded us to take over the departments in their other subsidiaries, including Kahns in Oakland and Rhodes in Tacoma. By the time this was finalized in 1952, we had also obtained a leased operation with Lou Johnson, a specialty store in Tacoma.

So in a relatively short time our business expanded a great deal. They provided the space and we paid them a percentage of every sale. We hired our own people, but the stores would meet the payroll and charge the amount back to us. Sometimes it worked well, sometimes it didn't, but it did help us control the shoe lines.

Our next leased operation was in Hawaii. Another subsidiary of AmFac, Liberty House, had a store on the main street in Honolulu and another in Waikiki, and we managed both shoe departments. Later, they built a store in the Ala Moana Shopping Center and we took over that shoe department as well.

Liberty House ended up expanding to the mainland by purchasing Western Department Stores, with stores in Albuquerque, Phoenix, Fresno, Sacramento and other cities. We ran the shoe departments in all of them for many years.

54

# Strike

WE were a union shop from the time my father and Mr. Wallin owned the business. My brothers and I felt that unions did a lot of good for employees by fighting for higher wages, shorter hours and more fringe benefits. This was especially true back in the old days when some stores barely paid a living wage. There were times, however, when we had our share of labor pains.

In 1932, the National Industrial Recovery Act (NIRA) was passed, giving unions more bargaining power during the Depression. At that time there was an attempt to establish maximum hours and minimum wages for shoe clerks in Seattle. A meeting was called and all the shoe store owners, perhaps fifteen of us, gathered to discuss the issues.

We were paying our sales people $25 for a work week of eight hours a day, six days a week. One store was paying $9.75 a week and most of the others paid around $12 a week. Naturally, they wanted the minimum wage set around their level. We tried to move them up, they tried to move us down. Finally we reached a compromise of a $17 minimum for a fifty-two hour week.

Ironically, our high pay scale put us on the front line when it came to battles with the union over negotiating contracts. The union figured that if we could be compelled to raise wages, then they could go to the other stores and say, "You'd better raise your wages. Just look at the contract we signed with Nordstrom's."

This happened the following year in 1933. The union representative arrived to present a new contract and I asked him how many stores had signed it. "None," he said. So I told him, "We're tired of always being first. Convince the other stores to sign, and we'll follow suit." A few days later he returned, but it was the same story. Not a single store was willing to sign.

It wasn't long afterward that a union picket showed up in front of our store. No one else's, just ours. The picket's sign said we were in violation of NIRA rules. We checked, and sure enough, there was a negotiating technicality in the NIRA rules that we weren't aware of. We were soon to find out, that meant big trouble.

We were taken to court, where we pleaded our case and lost. Convicted of a technicality, we were facing a stiff fine or even some time in jail, when the National Industrial Recovery Act was declared unconstitutional on May 27, 1934. The law was thrown out. We were saved by the bell.

Two decades passed without any major problems with the union. Then in 1954 came a real humdinger.

The union agent, Johnny Gentile, and I were engaged in negotiations over the next contract. He was a rough, tough fellow who pounded his fist on the table as we argued late into the night. A single issue was the big stumbling block. Our people were guaranteed $65.23 a week, and Gentile demanded that the work week be reduced from 44 hours to 40 hours with no reduction in pay.

We agreed to this demand for our stock clerks and other noncommission employees. However, we said our clerks on commission could work only 40 hours a week if they chose, but we would reduce their guarantee from $65.23 a week to $62 a week. The whole issue was pretty ridiculous anyway, since most of our people on commission were making anywhere from $85 to $115 a week.

During our talks, Johnny Gentile asked our employees for a strike authorization, claiming he would never use it. "If Elmer Nordstrom knows I have this authorization," he told them, "I can use it as a club." Our Seattle employees, about 100 strong, saw no harm in this and voted to affirm his power to call a strike. The next Monday afternoon, much to everyone's surprise, pickets appeared in front of our store. All the clerks nervously grabbed their hats and left, since in those days crossing a picket line was simply not done.

My brothers and I were shocked and angry. We thought negotiations were moving along, and that we already treated our employees as well as or better than any other store. Leaving work that evening, I ran into Johnny Gentile outside, and the two of us exchanged some strong language. He was smoking a cigarette, and in the heat of our discussion, he leaned up at me and blew smoke in my face. I grabbed his cigarette out of his mouth, tore it up and threw it back in his face. War was declared.

Inspired to fight this battle, we closed the Downtown store and mustered everyone in the family to keep the University and Northgate stores open for business. Our older children waited on customers, the younger ones handled stock work. Our wives changed money and wrapped purchases. We all pitched in to meet the challenge.

At one point, Johnny Gentile himself appeared in front of the University store carrying a picket sign. Since it was raining quite heavily, he parked himself in the foyer of the store to keep dry. Well aware of the laws governing the placement of pickets, Everett's wife Libby strode out to inform Gentile that he was on company property and therefore in violation of the law. She demanded he leave immediately. So he stepped out front and ducked under the awning. Everett chided Libby for being a little rough on the guy, then calmly walked outside to roll up the awning.

Our employees were pretty unhappy at being stuck with a strike they never wanted in the first place. One of our clerks took the risk of coming to the back door of the University store to keep us informed of developments. He said even the union members could get nowhere with Johnny Gentile. It looked like it was going to be a long and difficult strike. We prepared an advertisement for non-union help to re-open our Downtown store. Our people heard about it and we told them, "How many of you come back will depend on how good these new people are."

On July 1, the tenth day of the strike, forty-two of our employees met in the Labor Temple to protest Gentile's conduct and question the events that led to the strike. Chairman of the meeting was Arthur Gray, a clerk that had been with us for twenty-three years. He charged that an employer proposal on the day of the strike had not reached the union membership because "a certain individual did not agree with it." Gentile denied the claim, then added that he'd heard rumors that some of the members were thinking of joining the C.I.O. "If you do," Gentile warned, "you'd better plan to work for Nordstrom for life because you'll never work in another one of our stores."

"Nobody has mentioned the C.I.O.," Arthur Gray icily replied.

The next day, in spite of Gentile, the membership voted unanimously to return to work pending further negotiations. The strike had lasted eleven days and if anyone can win a strike, one could say that we won this one.

For the next three weeks we negotiated back and forth, with Gentile threatening to call another strike. Finally, we settled on a contract. The icing on the cake came when Gentile took this opportunity to announce that we were increasing our employer contributions to the health and welfare plan, an item that we brought to him in the early days of our talks.

All three brothers were involved from time to time in resolving our labor problems, but I was usually the one selected to act as the company representative, handling negotiations and taking the abuse. Looking back, I think our people would have done just as well without union intervention for the most part. Sometimes we were required to hold back raises and benefits until it was time for contract negotiations. And during negotiations we were forced to concede as little as possible, so that we would have some ammunition for the next bout.

A good example of this took place when we were ready to adopt our Profit Sharing Plan in 1956. Our attorney advised us to make an announcement to the union, and I arranged a meeting with Johnny Gentile to outline the details of the Plan. When I did, he frowned and asked how much the employees were required to contribute. I informed him it was completely employer-sustained, our employees wouldn't have to put in a single penny to enjoy the benefits. He seemed distressed. "I wish you wouldn't do this," he said. Surprised, I asked him why. "Because this should be the work of the union, and not come from management without a struggle."

Our Profit Sharing Plan was quite unique for the times. Not many plans even existed in those days. Sears was a notable exception, but their plan required employee contributions and ours did not. At first, profit sharing funds weren't made available until the employee turned sixty-five, but today, employees are vested after ten years with the company.

We created the Plan for two reasons. First of all, we employed sixty or seventy people at the time, knew them all on a first name basis and they were just like friends. It's extremely hard to retire people at sixty-five when there is nothing for them to fall back on and we wanted to make sure they were able to live comfortably when they retired.

Secondly, we felt the Plan would help us attract better personnel and indeed this was the case. It was a natural development that reflected our basic philosophy: the better we treated our people, the better our people performed. ✒

*The sales staff back in the old days.*

# Our People

OVER the years, my brothers and I worked with some top-notch people. We're proud that many chose to stay with the company for decades, while others did a good job for a short while before moving on to other positions. Sometimes, it seems as if half the attorneys in town sold shoes for us while going through law school. One of our clerks went on to become president of Boeing, another became president of the Prudential Life Insurance Company. And one of our elevator operators, Dyan Cannon, went on to become Mrs. Cary Grant and a fine actress in her own right.

They all contributed to the team effort. We wouldn't be where we are today without them.

In the early days, being a shoe clerk was not an enviable position. They were called "shoe dogs" and usually had no formal education. But they were fiery producers, tough guys, men who had to work hard to put bread on the table.

We never advertised for help, but applicants would appear because they knew with us they could make more money in sales commissions. Hiring them was usually a shot in the dark. In most cases we just looked them over, gave them a shoe horn and watched how they performed. It always helped to believe in them. Both Lloyd and Everett had a remarkable ability to instill confidence in people, and we all felt that if someone gave it their best, they would succeed.

Our buyers in those days were mainly old shoe salesmen who had worked their way up from the fitting stool. On buying trips to New York, Everett would gather his buyers together for early breakfast meetings. Looking around the table, there would be maybe fifteen men, one of whom had a college education. They were men who worked hard, and played hard. After a sixteen hour day with plenty of mental and physical strain, they tended to go out drinking. The next morning, when Everett was fresh after his eight hours of sleep, a lot of these men would be hung over and in pretty tough shape. But they all knew how important these meetings were and they all did their best to be sharp. At no time did any one of them stay in his room and tell Everett Nordstrom he couldn't make it that day.

Our clerks earned fixed salaries when we first started in business. Shortly thereafter we adopted a commissioned pay structure. It gave them added incentive to work harder, and by working harder, they were often able to build a loyal customer following. It was not unusual for our senior salesmen to sell almost all their shoes to customers who were waiting for them. The store could be filled, but they would all be people waiting for the special attention they received from their favorite salesman.

I remember one clerk from those days whose head was

as bald as an egg. At the time, women wore long skirts that had to be hoisted up a bit so that the salesman could fit shoes while leaning over a stool. One day this clerk was bent over adjusting the laces for a customer, when she glanced down and happened to see his bald head. She must have thought it was her knee, which under no circumstance could be allowed to show. So she pulled her skirts up, right over the surprised fellow's head.

We did everything we could to get the best people, and once we had them, we did everything we could to keep them. One of the things we believed in from the start was promoting from within. We wanted our people to know that they could work their way up, while also learning about the business on different levels.

Our strategy was simple. If a stock boy worked hard, we put him on the floor. If he (or she) sold well, he was made assistant manager. If that turned out well, he made manager. The principle worked well then and it works well today. Even the members of our own family know they have to start at the bottom like everyone else. Of course, not every salesperson makes a good manager, but almost every manager we ever had started on the sales floor.

We had a lot of contests to promote competition among our salespeople. For example, if we had too many red shoes, we would have a red shoe selling contest. In the early days we offered cash prizes to the top salesmen. Later it might be flowers, dinners or trips. In a sense, every day was a contest, because in the stock room there was a list of salesmen, ranked in order of their performance. Everyone tried to do their best, so that they wouldn't be stuck at the bottom of the list. Very rarely we would have a problem with someone trying to win outside the rules. There's a fine line between competition and non-cooperation, and we always watched to make sure no one crossed that line.

Company parties were one small way of showing our appreciation to our people. For years we would have everyone over to the family's summer place on Hood Canal for a picnic. As we grew, we moved the picnics to larger facilities like Beaver Lake by Issaquah. Those were fun times. There would be beer and food and plenty of games, and everyone enjoyed themselves with their families and co-workers. For our first Christmas parties we would bring out some drinks on Christmas Eve right after closing. That evolved into elaborate dinner/dances at places like the Spanish Ballroom in the Olympic Hotel for all our employees and their spouses.

On a day-to-day basis we tried to show our people that they were all members of a winning team. Occasionally, that meant going the extra mile to help someone out of a jam. I remember one young fellow we had working in the men's department, who, unknown to us, had borrowed money from a loan company and was paying an exorbitant amount of interest. The loan company came to me and wanted to garnishee his wages. I called the fellow up to my office and found out his child had some expensive medical problems. We loaned him money so he could pay off his debts, and so that he could relax a little and keep his mind on his job. He worked hard and paid us back every penny.

Another time, we had a boy working for us who got himself into a bad scrape and was sent to the penitentiary. When he got out he came to us and asked for a job, but he didn't even have a decent suit to wear to work. He came from a good family and wasn't a wild kid, so I talked it over with my brothers and said let's give him a chance. He was about my size, so I gave him a suit. He worked for us for years.

Some companies demand loyalty from personnel, but we felt that loyalty should come from us to them first. In any case, loyalty is something earned, not expected.

In a decentralized company such as ours, there is no one calling the shots from an ivory tower. We encourage our people to take the initiative and come up with ideas. They are given full authority as well as responsibility, and they know that they are being judged on their performance, not on how well they follow orders. They receive full credit when things go well, and when things don't, they have no one to blame but themselves. In this kind of environment, people strive to do their best.

My brother Everett gained a reputation as perhaps the most respected women's shoe buyer in the country. When he arrived in New York one year, all the shoe representatives were hovering around him. Everett just pointed to the young man who accompanied him and said, "Don't talk to me. This is my buyer." They all looked at this nervous twenty-two year old who was being put in charge of buying women's shoes, our biggest single buying job at the time. After that, the fellow worked his heart out for the company.

Our decentralized policy mystifies many experts. They claimed it would work well for a few stores, but as we expanded we would have to start issuing more direct orders from the top. As it turned out, our people proved them wrong.

*The three of us overseeing the remodeling of our Bellevue store.*

# The Secrets of Our Success

OF all the shoe stores in Seattle when Mr. Wallin and my father started theirs, ours is the only one left. How did we do it?

Many people think that we Nordstroms are secretive, because we don't talk much about ourselves. The truth is though, we can't afford to boast. If we did, we might start to believe our own stories, get big heads and stop trying.

However, just for the record, I'm going to let you in on the secrets of our success. They're very complicated, very confidential and, of course, I'm just joking. Our success is simply a matter of service, selection, fair pricing, hard work and plain luck.

Customer service has always been top priority. In our

estimation, the customer is always right. When we talk to our salespeople, we try to make them understand the importance of giving every customer extra attention, even the difficult ones.

I remember one salesman who came to work a little grumpy because he had a hard time with a customer the day before. I tried to explain my attitude to him. "You can wait on twenty customers and they are all friendly except one. So you might go home at night remembering only the bad one and forget about the nineteen who were so good. It should be the other way around."

In any business there is the occasional customer who is hard to please. One day many years ago, we had a burly lumberjack trying on shoes in our Downtown Seattle store. Our closing time was 6:00, but it got to be 6:15 and then 6:30. Everyone else had left but we needed to keep the cashier and clerk there until this fellow made up his mind. When it got near 7:00, I told the clerk to turn out the lights on the women's side to give our customer the hint, and then I went to do something else. When I returned, I saw that the clerk had turned out all of the lights in the store so that it was almost completely dark.

The lumberjack wasn't fazed at all. He just reached into his Mackinaw jacket and pulled out a flashlight. He didn't complain, he just kept shining it on one pair after another, trying to make up his mind. Finally, after a few more minutes, he said, "Well, I'll come back later."

My brothers and I always tried to be friendly and to say hello to customers in the store, calling them by name when we could. Even on the street we were in the habit of greeting people who looked at us, since they could be a customer and it never hurts to say hello. This boomeranged on me once as I was walking downtown. I noticed a fellow looking at me oddly as I approached, so as I got close I said, "Good morning." He grabbed me by the arm and said, "Do you know me?" Actually, I had never seen him before, but I gave it the old college try by saying, "Well, you look familiar—I'm just trying to place you." "That's funny," he replied, "I just arrived in town this morning from Chicago and I thought I didn't know a soul here."

Our reputation for carrying large sizes helped our business in a big way. This idea goes back to the days when my father and Mr. Wallin owned the store. Neither one knew much about merchandising when they opened, so they just ordered shoes in all the medium ranges. Soon they discovered that many of their friends who were big, tall Swedes couldn't find shoes large enough, and they began ordering larger sizes.

When my brothers and I bought the business we continued to carry up to size 18 for men and 13 for women. To order these sizes we had to approach manufacturers individually and convince them to purchase the equipment needed to craft larger shoes. Shoes are made over a "last," and each length and width in almost every style requires a special last. Since this equipment is expensive, we had to do a bit of persuading in the early years. Later, as our volume grew, the factories were happy to make the investment, especially because they could charge us more for larger sizes.

Though these large shoes cost us more, we always offered them at the same price or a fraction more than the regular sizes. It was good advertising. I remember traveling on a train and seeing a very tall man in the club car as I walked by. I would guess he wore a size 16. I overheard him say to his friends, "There are only two things I can buy ready made—neckties and shoes. I shop at Nordstrom's in Seattle."

I said one of the secrets of our success was fair pricing and it's true. If we have a reputation for being more expensive, it's only because we've tended to carry better lines. We worked on closer margins and never took as large a mark-up as our competitors. For that reason, other stores did not want to carry the same shoes as we did because they knew we would probably undersell them. If a customer came to us and said, "I can buy this for a better price at another store," we would meet the lower price. In fact, it rarely happened.

As the owners, we felt that we should work harder than anyone else. If we didn't, our lackadaisical attitude would spread to the next level, and the next level on down until everyone was taking it easy.

I remember talking to an acquaintance of mine, a jeweler, who would leave his business for long periods of time. I asked him if he was concerned about the possibility of setting a bad example. He replied that he had a way of dealing with that. "When I'm back in Seattle," he said, "I'm the busiest man around. My employees see me at my peak, but then I leave and take it easy again." It sounded like a tempting idea, but my brothers and I never tried it.

Perhaps we never did because from our experience during the war years, we saw how easily a business could fall apart from neglect. Years later, when we were getting ready to hand the business over to the next generation, we gave them a list of thirteen excuses. These included the weather, the economy, the new shopping center down the block, and so on. We told them they might as well give us their excuses by the number, because they didn't mean a thing. If business was bad, there was nowhere to put the blame but upon themselves.

Of course, no matter how hard you try, luck still plays a part in any business. It's impossible to accurately forecast trends every time. When we moved our Downtown store to Fifth Avenue from Second Avenue, we didn't know it would become one of the best locations in Seattle. When we opened our Northgate store, we didn't know that suburban shopping malls would become the wave of the future. On the other hand, when we bought the business we didn't know that the Depression was right around the corner.

Sometimes we were lucky, sometimes we weren't. But as luck would have it, most of the time we were, sometimes with success far beyond what we had envisioned.

# Expanding the Business

WE signed a lease that would double our Downtown Seattle store's floor space in 1957. Portland and Northgate were open and running, and at this point we had ten leased shoe departments. So we turned our efforts to expanding our home base.

With the new lease, we added more than 20,000 square feet by taking over the first three floors and basement of the Ranke Building. The following year we added even more street level space when Weisfield's Jewelry moved.

All of this took a lot of remodeling. We commissioned a tremendous pebble mural by artist Jean Johanson that weighed more than a ton. We gave everything a new, modern look. And in the basement, we installed our first "Shoe

69

Rack" with lower-priced shoes.

In March of 1959 we held a grand opening for our newly remodeled and expanded Downtown store. We could now claim to have the largest shoe store in the country. On four levels we carried over 100,000 pairs of shoes, including 150 sizes for women, 215 sizes for children, and 170 sizes for men.

While this was going on we also opened a store in Bellevue. The Eastside community was growing quickly and we saw an opportunity to serve an expanding market. For the grand opening we employed a publicity stunt that offered "your first shine free on that new pair of shoes." The store was a success from the day it opened.

We bought a store in Yakima in 1960. By 1961 we had opened a store in Lloyd Center outside Portland. In 1962 we added a store at Aurora Village.

The year of 1962 was a good one for Seattle businesses. The World's Fair opened and the city was flooded with visitors. My father was honored during "Sweden Week," and because of all the various festivities going on, the city played host to an unusual number of celebrities.

Johnny Mathis showed up at our Downtown store and all the girls went nuts. Another time, a funny little guy in a raincoat came running into the store carrying a pair of shoes. It was Colonel Tom Parker, Elvis Presley's manager. He told us Elvis was standing out in the Westlake Mall in his stocking feet, surrounded by girls. His shoes had come apart and they weren't "blue suede shoes" either, just a pair of cheap, pointed boots that had split open on the sides. We took them down to our shoe repair department and gave them V.I.P. treatment. You couldn't have the King of Rock'n Roll walking around outside Nordstrom's without a pair of shoes. It wouldn't look right.

A couple of years earlier when we opened our Yakima store, we had an incident which tested the mettle of some of our younger employees. It makes a pretty good story.

We had a promising young assistant manager at our Northgate store and we decided to make him the manager of a shoe store in Yakima that we had just purchased. It was an old style store, with tall ladders for reaching shoes that were stacked to the ceiling. We were able to lease the space next door to it, and our new manager went to work remodeling and getting ready for a grand opening.

For years we had monkeys in cages in the children's shoe departments of our stores. The managers weren't happy about it, but the children loved them. So when we remodeled the Yakima store, we included an air-conditioned cage in the design, and ordered two monkeys months in advance.

For the grand opening we publicized a "Name the Monkeys" contest for children under fourteen. But with only one week to go, we hadn't received our monkeys. Then, two days before the opening date, our agent called and said, "I'm afraid I won't be able to supply your monkeys in time."

That put us in a real fix. With all the publicity, we had to have those monkeys for the opening. Luckily, our Yakima manager had a brother and a friend who worked at our Bellevue store, both of whom were planning to drive to Yakima that evening to help out the next day. It was suggested that they bring along two monkeys from the Bellevue store, and they agreed.

Now, as an older man, I think I can get away with the privilege of being a little vague on names at times, so I'll just call the brother and his friend, Jim and Jack.

After Bellevue closed at 6:00, Jim and Jack found a large cardboard box and got ready to transfer the monkeys from their cages into this carrier. However, these monkeys had lived in their cages for quite some time and were no longer cute, little fellows—they were big, tough and shrewd. So as soon as the cage was opened, they zipped out past Jim and Jack and ran all over the store, climbing curtains and hanging from the ceiling.

The boys tried for hours to catch them without success. Near midnight, they called another employee who had become friendly with the monkeys over the years, and he came down to the store and coaxed them into the box with food. Jim and Jack shoved the box into the trunk of the car, picked up their wives and set out for Yakima.

It took them all night to cross the mountains because of a terrific snowstorm. For hours they sat in the car, inching their way along the pass, worried about the health of the monkeys in the trunk. When they finally arrived in the early morning, the monkeys were fine. They were so tough, none of this bothered them. So they transferred the monkeys into their new cage, checked into a motel and slept right through the grand opening. To top it off, the other monkeys arrived that morning anyway.

Despite all that monkeying around, all three of those boys have done well with the company. For those of you who haven't guessed the punch line already, the promising young manager in the story was my son, John. And the brother and his friend were, in fact, named Jim and Jack. They're my son, Jim, and Lloyd's son-in-law, Jack McMillan.

*Best's Apparel at Fifth and Pine around 1950.*

# Getting into Apparel

$B$Y the early 1960s, it was apparent that we had grown about as much as we could with shoes in the Pacific Northwest. So we were faced with an important decision. We could move into California with our own shoe stores, not leased operations, or we could expand in the Northwest by moving into the apparel business.

When we studied the figures, it was obvious that getting into apparel was the better course. However, to start from scratch would be difficult. We decided to try taking over an existing operation in order to give us an opportunity to learn the industry.

Dorothy Cabot Best was a leading retail fashion figure in Seattle for the first half of this century. She and her husband

73

Ivan had a shop on Third Avenue and then later moved their business, Best Apparel, into a building on Fifth and Pine. This building had been transformed earlier from an old theater into an apparel store by Livingston's, a San Francisco company, which lasted only six years in Seattle because of the Depression. The Bests bought the site, rebuilt it and continued to enjoy an excellent reputation for high quality women's apparel. Dorothy was often quoted in the news-papers as an authority on fashion, and she orchestrated the finest fashion shows in Seattle.

When Mrs. Best passed away, the running of the store was assumed by her husband, who was a financial man and not prepared to handle the merchandising aspects of the business. Without Dorothy Best, the family lost their enthu-siasm and business slowly declined. So when we approached Mr. Best with our interest in buying his store, he was very receptive.

This was a big move for us, and for him, and negotia-tions went on for years. Lloyd, though, was one of the most patient negotiators in the world. He seemed to want this move even more strongly than Everett and I. Perhaps it was because he was the youngest, and came into the business without cost after we had already put five years into it. Some people remembered this and thought Lloyd was less than a full partner, which wasn't true. But knowing that some people thought that, perhaps made Lloyd want to become the driving force behind our new venture. Whatever the reason, he stuck with it until he had worked out a beneficial agreement for all.

On the day Mr. Best agreed to the terms, Everett and Lloyd called me. I was up in Canada on a boating trip. As soon as I heard they were ready to sign, I took an opposing position, something one of us often did just to be able to see all sides of an issue. I said, "Are we sure about this? We don't really know a lot about apparel. Maybe we should stay with shoes."

There was a moment's hesitation on the other end of

the line, and then I heard Lloyd, who had worked so long and so hard to put it all together, say, "If you don't think we should, we won't." But of course, we did. We all just wanted to make sure that we were ready to tackle this new project without reservations as a team.

The sale was announced on August 6, 1963. The take-over went smoothly; Ivan Best retired and Lloyd moved over to manage the operations. We were now in the apparel business.

Many people in Seattle thought we were making a big mistake. Even the newspapers wrote us off. No one really believed that shoe store owners could be successful with apparel. No one, except us. We sharpened our pencils and tackled the budgets, working our inventory department by department. And we found we could buy and sell apparel. It's true, the manufacturers weren't very enthused to see us on buying trips, but that only reminded us of our early days in shoes. It was like starting over in many ways, and that was exciting.

Lloyd instituted changes immediately. Mr. Best had run the store in a very formal manner. According to an unwritten rule, employees couldn't talk to him unless he said hello first. That made for a lot of quiet rides in the elevator. Lloyd always greeted all the employees by name when he walked through the store. His management style created a whole new atmosphere.

He also began updating Best Apparel's image. When they started out, they were an ultra-modern store with a young clientele. But as time went by, they grew old with their established customers until they were offering clothing that appealed mostly to mature women. Consequently, they were not gaining any new customers and the ones they had were slowly disappearing. It was natural when we took over to transform the operation to appeal to a younger group of consumers, the Baby Boom generation. We added juniors and sportswear because we knew that there would be a lot of younger business on the way.

Lloyd was a man of vision, with an extraordinary sense of leadership. As active head, he rearranged the management structure, while retaining some of Best's top personnel. As he needed new help, he went outside our organization for experienced apparel buyers and managers. However, within two years, most of his people were home-trained. It turned out that those who had started on the floor selling shoes ended up being the best at selling apparel. Stanley Marcus of Neiman Marcus once said that it was his background in shoes that made him a successful merchant. If someone can work with shoes, then apparel is easy.

In a short time, our "big mistake" began to look more like a real bonanza.

More than 1000 men jammed Nordstrom Best women's store in Seattle, in a shopping spree "for men only" promoted via radio spots on KVI Seattle. As evidenced here, it's not at all certain whether the men are admiring the model or the peignoir she's demonstrating for their avid approval. Hardwick, disc jock for KVI, is likewise demonstrating his sales powers.

# Grand Openings

I N 1964, we announced plans to open a new Best Apparel at Northgate, adjacent to our existing Nordstrom's shoe store. We decided to design the stores to match and make it easy for shoppers to go from one to the other. Ironically, the original plans for Northgate in 1946 had included a proposed site for Best Apparel.

All three of us were heavily involved with the plans, but as construction began, I assumed control of getting the job done. The plans called for a special tile floor at street level. These tiles were created for us by a factory in California, and when they arrived right on schedule, the crews started laying them. However, when a quarter of the floor had been covered, the edges of the twelve-by-six inch tiles all began to curl up.

We discovered that there was something defective in

the mix of the tiles and there wasn't time to correct it before our scheduled opening date. We quickly began contacting carpet manufacturers round the country, trying to find one who could supply us with the right amount of quality carpeting in a very short time. We found one in North Carolina, and they began to send us a few rolls at a time.

The opening date kept getting closer. Soon we were having the carpets flown in by air right out of the mill. Rolls would arrive by Flying Tiger in the middle of the night and the supervisor of the carpet laying operation would meet the plane, bring back the rolls, have them installed, then wait for the next delivery. At one point, a heavy snowstorm forced our plane to drop its shipment in Sparks, Nevada. It wasn't easy getting a carpet from Sparks to Northgate, but we did, just in time for our grand opening on February 1, 1965.

In the following January, we purchased a Portland retail fashion outlet, Nicholas Ungar. We merged that store with our Downtown Portland store, and for the first time, customers were greeted by a new name—Nordstrom Best.

Meanwhile, we were gearing up for a new, combined Nordstrom's and Best Apparel in Tacoma.

The grand opening took place on August 5, 1966. There were 45,000 square feet on two floors, and the store resembled a collection of elegant boutiques. We developed a cruciform floor plan that had men's, women's and children's sections around a central, skylighted area for accessories. For the first time, our men's wear department carried a complete selection of suits, sportcoats, furnishings and sportswear. The store was instantly successful.

For Christmas that year we dreamed up a publicity stunt to bring more men into our Downtown Seattle store for the holidays. Women were by far our biggest group of customers, but we wanted to show Seattle men that we now offered clothing for them, as well as help them choose presents for the women in their lives. So we promoted a "Men Only" night.

At our regular 6:00 closing time, our people escorted all the women out of the store and locked the doors. Shortly afterward we reopened the store and allowed only men to enter. There were over 1,500 just waiting to get in. Inside, they were treated to fashion shows, and pretty models helped them to choose their gifts. Other models guided them through our Gentlemen's Shop. The whole affair was so low-key and soft-sell that many men asked timidly if they could buy something.

In 1967, we officially changed our name in Washington to Nordstrom Best. We employed 2,500 people, including part-time college students, in shoe stores, apparel stores and nineteen leased shoe departments. Things were looking good, and there was more to come.

The grand opening of our newly remodeled Nordstrom Best in Bellevue was in November of 1967. The main attraction was a so-called "magic staircase." Our architect designed a curving staircase with scarlet carpeting that rose on pillars from a pool sparkling with a fountain and flood lights. Suspended between the staircase and the skylight dome was supposed to be a spectacular chandelier. Our architect told us about one crafted in Germany that was hanging in the Joseph Magnin store in Glendale. So on my next trip to California, I took some pictures of it. Then we had a local craftsman create one for us, which saved both time and money.

It was our practice before grand openings to hold a preview party to benefit various non-profit community groups. We would buy refreshments, then the group would sell tickets to the party, with all the proceeds going to the worthy cause they represented. The party for this opening benefited a local Bellevue organization, the Overlake Memorial Hospital Auxiliaries.

Well, this night, the party was supposed to be over at at 9:00. When it got to be that time, our store operator announced on the public address system, "It's nine o'clock now, we're closing, thank you for coming." Everyone started to leave, and soon there were only two men left.

I had noticed these men when they arrived. They appeared to have started their partying pretty early. By 9:30

they still hadn't made any sign of leaving, so I went up to meet them on the magic staircase. "Gentlemen," I said, "it was nice to have you here, but it's close to 10:00 now, and we would like to close the store so we can go have our dinner."

One of the two stood up straighter and looked me in the eye, saying, "You don't know who I am, do you?" "Why no," I replied, "I don't." "Well," he continued, "I'm Jim Nordstrom." "Oh?" I said, "I'm very pleased to meet you. I'm your father."

As they turned and slunk away, we had a pretty good chuckle.

In 1968, we had the grand opening of our Nordstrom Best store at Southcenter. It was even bigger than our Downtown store, and was our first store with escalators. The preview party for this event benefited Children's Orthopedic Hospital.

Once again I had been put in charge of supervising construction. The architectural plans called for carpeting and it was installed without incident. However, one week before the opening, I received a call at 2:00 in the morning from the fire department, informing me that the sprinklers had accidentally gone off.

I left immediately for the store and found that our floor was covered with several inches of water. The carpet company representative arrived soon after, and had some men remove the soaking carpet and take it back to their facility to dry it out. A few days later, the carpet was back down on the floor even though it had shrunk a bit. Just before the opening date, I received another early morning call: the sprinklers again. This time a good deal of merchandise was soaked.

Another time, the fire department called, again in the middle of the night, to say that the basement of our Downtown store was being flooded by our sprinklers.

Whenever this happened, my wife would be concerned about me going down to a dark, deserted store alone at night. She would ask, "Are you sure it's an honest call?"

They were all honest calls, though. They were an honest pain in the neck.

*John, Jim and Bruce. A new generation of Nordstroms takes over.*

# Handing Over the Reins

I N 1968 Everett turned sixty-five. Many years earlier we
decided that each of us would retire when we reached that
age. Everett, Lloyd and I always believed that if the business
was to succeed, we would have to retire at an earlier age than
we might have liked. Our decision came from our observa-
tions of other companies.

Too often we saw businesses fail because they were run
by an older member who refused to relinquish his position.
Many times as the founder of a business grows old, his
thinking becomes more inclined towards security, and risks
are avoided that might have led to growth. Employees won't
find much incentive for coming up with new ideas if they
know they'll be viewed as too risky by an older, conservative

81

boss. The result is sometimes an old taskmaster, surrounded by "Yes-Men," rather than people who want to take charge and produce.

My father retired at fifty-eight and gave us our chance. Now our turns were coming up, even though we were in good health and capable of continuing. The trouble was, since most of our equity was tied up in the company, we had nothing to retire on.

We never paid ourselves dividends from the business because we always wanted to use that money for further expansion. The three of us would simply draw out enough money to live on, and we watched ourselves to make sure we all received the same salary each year. Now we were facing a situation when our income would stop. Selling out to one of the larger retail companies was an obvious option, and once we made our intentions known, we received quite a bit of interest.

We informed three companies that we would listen to their offers. Edward Carter of Carter-Hawley-Hale was our first visitor. His offer was not that far off and we knew it would be improved. At this point, we approached the third generation with the news of this offer. But it turned out, they had some ideas of their own.

For the most part I've avoided talking about the third generation of Nordstroms so far, but the truth is, with every passing year, their importance was growing as members of the team.

Everett's son Bruce and my sons John and Jim all started doing tasks at the store when they were only nine years old. At first we just paid them out of our own pockets rather than put them on the payroll.

One summer when they were teenagers, John and Jim decided they wanted to try something new. That was fine with me since I knew they were trying to prove themselves. John got a job gassing boats on Lake Union and came home every night covered with grease. Jim went to work for a nursery and once he said, "I can't understand it. Every time I have to push a wheelbarrow full of manure, it's uphill." The next summer they both came back to work at Nordstrom's.

By 1966, Bruce had worked his way up to vice-president of merchandising for shoes. John also had become a vice-president, and so had Lloyd's son-in-law Jack McMillan, who began selling shoes for us while he was in college. The next year, Jim became vice-president of merchandising for sportswear and junior apparel.

When we told them that we were thinking of selling out, they told us they could do a better job of running the company than any outside organization. But my brothers and I had our doubts. After all, the main reason we did so well was our ability to work together as a cohesive unit. We didn't know if the boys could do that, and we didn't want to see them break up into feuding factions trying to. We were unsure of which course to take.

The decision hung in the air for a while, and then the third generation found a way to convince us they could get along with each other and run the business. They came to us with an outline, a game plan, and held a candid discussion on their strengths and weaknesses, describing all the pros and cons.

They made a good presentation and we were impressed. It was apparent that they were enthusiastic and that their dedication was equal to the task. So we began to rethink our position. Even so, as my nephew Bruce put it, our decision was "a roll of the dice."

We decided to call Mr. Carter and tell him we had changed our minds. Then we called the other two firms and told them to cancel their plans to visit us, since we would be turning over the business to the third generation. It turned out to be the better decision. The total market value of our company today after fifteen years is over thirty times greater than what we would have sold it for to Carter-Hawley-Hale.

In a recent talk with my son Jim, he told me, "Our pro forma from our presentation, which I still have, estimated that we would reach $100 million in sales by 1980 . . . and you didn't think we would make it." In 1980, Nordstrom sales reached almost half a billion dollars.

However, not selling out meant that we would have to go public for the first time since the beginning of the company. That was quite a change for us since we were used to keeping quiet about our business. But we had to issue the stock in order to provide security for our retirement.

In June of 1971, each of us sold 147,000 shares which represented one-third of our individual holdings. The Nordstrom family retained seventy-nine percent of the company.

The stock sold out in one day. Our employees had the opportunity to buy stock a few points under the selling price, and a few of them did. We didn't encourage them to buy, but as it turned out, buying that stock would have been a very good investment.

By March of 1970, the reins were firmly in the hands of the third generation: Bruce A. Nordstrom, thirty-seven; James F. Nordstrom, thirty; John N. Nordstrom, thirty-three; and John A. McMillan, thirty-nine.

Here I must mention someone special the third generation added to their team, Robert Bender. Bob is the first executive in our company who is not a family member. He is an important asset to Nordstrom and shares merchandising responsibilities with Bruce, Jim, John and Jack.

My brothers and I became co-chairmen of the board, offering encouragement and resisting the temptation to give advice. The boys continued an aggressive growth program and when we urged caution, we were usually overruled. 🖋

*A 1985 photo of the new Nordstrom Tower addition to Swedish Hospital.*

# Community Involvement

ONCE the third generation took charge of the business in 1970, my brothers and I had more time to pursue our other interests. We had all been members of various clubs and organizations, such as the Seattle Golf Club, the Seattle Yacht Club, the Rainier Club and the Washington Athletic Club, but most of our time was spent dealing with the business.

With our company responsibilities lightened, Lloyd was free to go after the Seahawks, Everett could spend more time traveling and golfing, and I could use the opportunity to continue my efforts on the board of Swedish Hospital.

My wife's father founded the Swedish Hospital in 1908. Shortly after I was married in 1934, I was placed on the board.

85

It was a non-salaried, voluntary position and, like all other board members, I was simply making a contribution as a civic duty.

Dr. N. A. Johanson, my father-in-law, was a surgeon who more or less ran the hospital by himself in the early days. There were no staff organizations and carefully planned administrations. So when he passed away in 1945, the board was without leadership and I was chosen to become president.

It was rough for a while, since we had to find and hire one administrator after another to take over all the areas that my father-in-law had controlled himself. But we had dedicated hospital employees who deserve a major share of the credit for making our efforts a success. We also had good people on the board who used their professional skills and business sense to create a smooth running operation.

Working on the board demanded the ability to deal with a rapidly changing scope in hospital care. For instance, shortly after the war, a stay in the hospital cost around $15 a day. Now that cost is well over $500 a day. From the start, we knew we had to treat the hospital as a business, even though it is a non-profit organization.

Our objective wasn't to make money, but to make it possible for the hospital to continue to grow without financial difficulties. We didn't rely on community funding as many other hospitals traditionally have done. Instead, we created a profitable facility, with the profits going into better service, better personnel and a better method of serving our community.

Over the years our strategy showed good results. By the time I retired as an active board member, Swedish Hospital covered nine blocks, employed 2,700 people and had become the largest hospital in the Northwest.

Of course, my efforts were only those that any businessman could make. We had many talented individuals who made outstanding contributions. No doubt a fellow board member, John Soderberg, alluded to that fact one day on an outing on my boat. I had just had an operation where blood transfusions were donated by all the members of the board. As he put it, "You've certainly improved your standards, now that you have the blood of twelve good men flowing in your veins."

It wasn't long after we retired from the business that my brothers and I were able to make a civic contribution in a different vein. It was one of our last major projects for the company, and one that pumped new life-blood straight into the heart of downtown Seattle.

In 1971, a billboard appeared that said, "Will the last person leaving Seattle please turn out the lights." A severe economic recession was firmly in place, the Boeing company almost went under, unemployment was as high as twenty percent and Nordstrom continued to expand.

In between our shoe operation in the Ranke building on Pike and our apparel business in the Best building on Pine was the Gottstein building. We were able to buy it and set about tearing it down in September of that year. We had big plans for Seattle at a time when "Going out of business" or "Moving to the suburbs" signs were cropping up all around.

At an auction that benefited PONCHO, a local charitable organization, the highest bidder bought one hour at the controls of the wrecking ball. When he missed on a swing and slammed into the Best building just below Jim's office, the fellow quit before his time was up, saying, "It's harder than it looks."

And so were our big plans. Since we were determined to keep our stores open during construction and remodeling, the operation required complicated scheduling and precise execution. It would have been a nightmare, but we managed to do it in phases.

John supervised construction and I assisted him because of my experience. In Phase One we rebuilt over the destroyed Gottstein building. In Phase Two we tore down the Best building when we found out it would be too expensive to bring it up to code. In Phase Three we rebuilt over the

Best building site. And in Phase Four we strengthened and remodeled the Ranke building. Finally, with Phase Five, we changed the name of the company officially from Nordstrom Best to Nordstrom.

The project ended up costing us almost twice what we thought it would. But when we were finished, we had a superb new 230,000 square foot store and corporate headquarters that stretched for an entire block along Fifth Avenue. And Seattle had its first major downtown retail project in over a decade—a project that helped restore confidence and spark downtown redevelopment at a time when things were pretty grim.

In July of 1973, our project was completed. Unfortunately, my brother Everett saw only part of the results. He passed away on July 1, 1972, following a heart attack on a golf course.

He was missed and eulogized by many. The newspapers reported he was, "One of the founders of the Downtown Business Association, constant supporter of the University of Washington and the Beta Theta Pi Fraternity, intensely loyal friend, successful businessman, rabid sports fan, a competitor and a man whose entire life was a study in determination."

They could have added that he was a great man, and an even greater older brother.

*Lloyd Nordstrom and Pete Rozelle of the National Football League.*

# Heaven and Hell in the NFL

*L* LOYD should be the one to write this chapter. It was Lloyd who orchestrated the Nordstrom involvement with the Seattle Seahawks, who spearheaded the community movement to build the Kingdome, who helped bring a professional football franchise to our city. It was Lloyd who became known in 1974 as "Mr. Fifty-One Percent."

Even in his sixties, Lloyd was still a young man with a lot of energy when he left the company in the hands of the third generation. When he heard that the NFL was going to award a franchise to Seattle, he thought he would like to have a part of it, maybe ten percent. Lloyd was on the board of the Westin Hotel and joined a group of several businessmen there who also had a desire to secure an interest in

89

the franchise.

However, it wasn't that easy. The NFL insisted that one person be a majority owner and hold a fifty-one percent interest. Finding one person with that much money was difficult, though, because the asking price for the franchise was several million dollars.

So Lloyd wrangled approval from the NFL to have our family, as a closely held group, take the fifty-one percent. Then he began lining up support among the Nordstroms.

When he first approached me, I declined. I felt it wasn't a very good investment, especially for a man of my age, because there would be very little return on the money. The younger generation was very enthused and with their help, Lloyd got close to making the deal. But not close enough.

That's when he came back to talk with me, saying that he couldn't do it without my support. Even my son John who at first had also declined had now come around to Lloyd's way of thinking. With the rest of the team all lined up, I decided it was time to punt and agreed to join. And the Nordstrom family became majority owners of the Seahawks.

Lloyd was excited about being part of professional football, but he also felt he was doing a public service by bringing a team to Seattle that was under the ownership of local people. The city's other major league teams at the time were all owned by people who lived elsewhere. Other local businessmen also pitched in to fill out the roster, and they included Herman Sarkowsky, Ned Skinner, Howard Wright, Lynn Himmelman and Monte Bean.

But just when everything was going well, Lloyd passed away from a heart attack on a tennis court in Mexico after a football meeting in Miami. That was a sad day. He was one of the city's great supporters and was eulogized by everyone from businessmen, civic leaders and sports fans alike. Many of our employees took the news especially hard. He was their champion and will be missed for a long time to come.

After Lloyd's passing, the other members of the family

voted to keep his interest in the family by dividing it equally among the eight of us. Maybe because I was the oldest, but probably because I was the least busy, I was asked to be the spokesman for the family and represent us all as majority stockholder.

As the family spokesman, I have gotten to know the players. Since Kitty and I travel with them to most of the away games, we sit with them on the airplane and on the buses that carry the team back and forth. I make it a practice to visit the locker room after the games, congratulating our players when it's called for and commiserating with them when things don't go so well.

# New Recruits

I am now the last surviving member of our original team. My health is good and hopefully I'll be around for many years to come. Meanwhile, the team has grown. In fact, there are so many new family members that people outside the family sometimes have trouble keeping track of us all. So I thought it would be useful to provide a family tree, generation by generation.

**The first generation**—my father John W. Nordstrom and his wife Hilda Carlson.

**The second generation**—Everett and Elizabeth "Libby" Jones; Lloyd and Illsley Ball; my sister Esther and her husband Lawrence Smith; myself and Katherine "Kitty" Johanson. Another sister, Mabel, died as a teenager in 1919.

**The third generation**—Everett and Libby had two children; Bruce and Anne. Bruce married Fran Wakeman, who passed away, and Anne is married to Wayne Gittinger.

Lloyd and Illsley had three girls; Loyal, Linda and Susan. Loyal is married to John McMillan, Linda was married to David Mowat, and Susan is married to Richard Eberhart.

Esther, who passed away, and Lawrence Smith had three children; Marilyn, David and Lawrence Jr. (who also passed away). Marilyn is married to Don Gamble, David is married to Carol Kennel and Lawrence Jr. was married to Melanie.

Kitty and I have two boys, John and Jim. John is married to Sally Boid and Jim is married to Sally Anderson.

**The fourth generation**—Bruce has three boys; Blake, Peter and Erik. Anne's children are John and Susan.

Loyal and John McMillan's children are Keri, John, Laurie, Wendy and David. Linda's children are Kimberly, David, Mark, and Mari. Susan and Richard Eberhart's children are Elise, Ricky, Paul, Michael, Sara and Susan.

Marilyn and Don Gamble's children are Kim, Larry and Don Jr. The children of David Smith are Karen, Kristen and

Kellen. Lawrence Jr. and Melanie's son is Lawrence K. III.

John and Sally have three children; Kristin, James and John. The children of Jim and Sally are Daniel, William, Charles and James Jr.

As more members of the fourth generation grow up and marry, I'm sure new generations will be added to the team. In the meantime, the third generation has been doing an outstanding job. Because of their efforts and their ability to work together, Nordstrom has become the talk of the industry.

Bruce, Jim, John and Jack have kept our decentralized style of management and many new people have joined and been promoted within the company. In 1985, sales surpassed Saks Fifth Avenue, making Nordstrom the largest specialty store chain in the country. I only regret that my brothers are not here to see their success.

I'm sure Everett and Lloyd would have agreed that we left the company in good hands.

That pretty well wraps up our story. The next one is theirs.

*Elmer J. Nordstrom*

Seattle, 1986

# A Family Scrapbook

Here are some of our favorite snapshots showing how the family has grown.

*Father with his grandchildren. Bottom row, l. to r.—Jim, Linda, Susan, Loyal and Anne Nordstrom. Top row, l. to r.—John and Bruce Nordstrom; Larry, David and Marilyn Smith (Esther's children).*

*Together with our wives during an outing on my boat, l. to r.—Kitty, me, Illsley, Libby, Lloyd and Everett.*

---

*A formal family portrait taken at the opening of our Northgate store. Bottom row, l. to r.—Kitty, me, Libby, Everett, Illsley and Lloyd. Top row, l. to r.— Jim, Sally, John, Sally, Bruce, Fran, Anne, Don, Susan, Richard, Loyal, Jack, Linda and David.*

*Most of the fourth generation gathered together. Seated, l. to r.—Charlie, David, Michael, Ricky, Wendy, Mari, John II, Jim Jr., David, Paul and Mark. Standing, l. to r.—Bill, Pete, Kristie, Dan, Kim, Laurie, Erik, Susan, Kristen, Jim, Keri, John and Blake.*

---

*Bruce's family, l. to r.—Erik, Pete, Fran, Blake and Bruce.*

John's family, l. to r.—Jim, John II, Sally, John and Kristie.

Jim's family, l. to r.—Bill, Jamie, Charlie, Sally, Jim and Dan.

*Loyal's family, l. to r.—Keri, Loyal (Nordstrom) McMillan, Jack, Laurie, David, Wendy. Not shown—John.*

---

*Susan's family, l. to r.—Sara, Susan (Nordstrom) Eberhart, Richard, Elise, Paul, Michael and Rick.*

*Anne's family, l. to r.—Susan, Wayne, Anne (Nordstrom) Gittinger and John.*

*Linda's family, seated, l. to r.—David, Linda Nordstrom and Kimberly. Standing, l. to r.—Mark and Mari.*

ACKNOWLEDGMENTS

I wish to thank the many people who helped in the preparation of this book. This includes members of my family, relatives and people in our organization who provided a wealth of facts, details and photographs; John Koval who assisted me in the early stages; David Horsfall who helped with the final draft; and Terri Nakamura who provided the graphic design.